From ourSide of the Fence

Growing Up in America's
Concentration Camps

From our Side of the Fence

Growing Up in America's Concentration Camps

Edited by
Brian Komei Dempster

Produced by
Japanese Cultural &
Community Center of
Northern California

Published by
Kearny Street Workshop

Major funding for this publication provided by the
California Civil Liberties Public Education Program

Editor: Brian Komei Dempster
Book Designer: Zand Gee
Director of Programs/JCCCNC: Jill Mari Shiraki

Cover illustration, "Childhood Dreams" © 1983 Ruth Y. Okimoto. Color and
graphite pencil on paper, 27 x 30 in. Courtesy of Mrs. Heizo Oshima.
Aerial photo of the Topaz War Relocation Center, 1943, by a Topaz internee.

All written material is previously unpublished except for the following works:
an excerpt of Kiku Hori Funabiki's "Silence . . . No More" originally appeared in
Teacher's Guide: The Bill of Rights and the Japanese American World War II Experience.
San Francisco: National Japanese American Historical Society, 1992: 44;
Sato Hashizume's "The Food" originally appeared in *Only What We Could Carry:
The Japanese American Internment Experience*, edited by Lawson Fusao Inada et al.
Berkeley: Heyday Books, 2000: 109.

Printing by Inkworks Press, Berkeley, California, U.S.A.

Library of Congress Cataloging-in-Publication Data
      From our side of the fence : growing up in America's
concentration camps / edited by Brian Komei Dempster.
         p. cm.
      "Produced by Japanese Cultural & Community Center of Northern
California."
      Includes bibliographical references.
         ISBN 0-9705504-0-5
         1. Japanese Americans—Evacuation and relocation, 1942-1945.
      2. World War, 1939-1945—Japanese Americans—Biography. 3.
      World War, 1939-1945—Personal narratives, American. 4.
      Concentration camps—United States—History—20th century. I.
      Dempster, Brian Komei, 1969- II. Japanese Cultural & Community
      Center of Northern California.
         D769.8.A6 F76 2001
         940.54'7273—dc21

2001001859

Produced by Japanese Cultural & Community Center of Northern California
For orders and information contact:
JCCCNC, 1840 Sutter Street, San Francisco, CA 94115
Tel: 415-567-5505; Fax: 415-567-4222; www.jcccnc.org

Published by Kearny Street Workshop
934 Brannan Street, San Francisco, CA 94103
Tel/Fax: 415-503-0520; www.kearnystreet.org

2nd Printing, 2003

For our parents,
our families,
and generations to come

Contents

Chiura Obata, "Talking Through the Wire Fence," Tanforan, July 1942.
Sumi on paper, 11 x 15.75 in. Courtesy of the Obata family.

Preface

The collection of stories, *From Our Side of the Fence*, attests to how the Japanese American community has endured. Despite the harsh external forces of racism, economic oppression, and wartime hysteria during World War II, the community found strength to rebuild and renew itself *kodomo no tame ni*, for the sake of the children. These stories share life in America's concentration camps as the writers remember them, capturing their experiences of childhood and youth.

In December 1941, Japan bombed Pearl Harbor. In the ensuing weeks, Japanese Americans were accused of harboring loyalties to Japan and became the targets of suspicion and racial hatred. The U.S. Justice Department singled out the first-generation Issei who had high standing and influence in their communities—some of these leaders were the writers' parents. Though the FBI ransacked their homes for radios, weapons, and any other item they could use to build a case against the Issei for sabotage and espionage against the United States, not a single shred of actual evidence was found to support these charges.

Nonetheless, these Issei were rounded up by the FBI and taken away from their families. On February 19, 1942, President Roosevelt signed Executive Order 9066 into law. This mandated the uprooting of over 120,000 Japanese Americans from their homes, among them the writers in this book.

For San Francisco's Japantown, a community that has been uprooted three times over[1], the Japanese Cultural & Community Center of Northern California (JCCCNC) was envisioned by the Nisei (second-generation Japanese Americans) as a home for the community that could not be taken away. In providing a space for the community to gather, struggle, grieve, create, grow, and renew itself, the JCCCNC, modeled by the generations before us, meets its call to the future. The student writers in the Internment Autobiography Writing Workshop, led by Brian Komei Dempster, discovered that here, they could freely explore and express their camp experiences.

This anthology is comprised of the stories of eleven student writers:

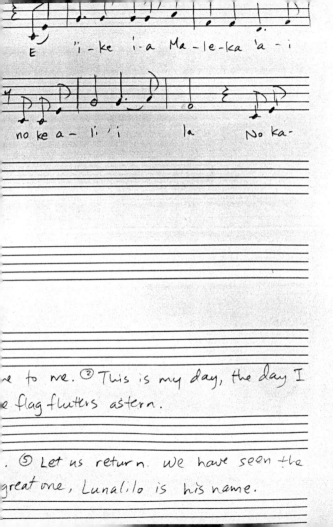

E   'i-ke i-a Ma-le-ka 'a-i

no ke a-li'i   la   No ka-

...e to me. ② This is my day, the day I
...e flag flutters astern.

... ⑤ Let us return. We have seen the
great one, Lunalilo is his name.

Florence Ohmura Dobashi, Kiku Hori Funabiki, Sato Hashizume, Fumi Manabe Hayashi, Florence Miho Nakamura, Ruth Y. Okimoto, Yoshito Wayne Osaki, Toru Saito, Daisy Uyeda Satoda, Harumi Serata, and Michi Tashiro. Before World War II, they lived in locations spanning the entire West Coast, including Washington, Oregon, the San Francisco Bay Area, the San Joaquin Valley, the Sacramento Valley, and Southern California. Ranging in age from four to nineteen at the outset of their incarceration, they were interned in six of the ten camps created by the War Relocation Authority: Amache, Heart Mountain, Minidoka, Poston, Topaz, and Tule Lake.

The lesson plans for Dempster's Internment Autobiography Writing Workshop contain the class assignments from which most of the student writings emerged. These sixteen lessons provide a clear and structured model for any internee who wishes to record his or her wartime memories. Through examples and vignettes of the classroom experience, and an examination of different techniques the writers used, the introductory material to the lesson plans offers a valuable "how to" guide on approaching the challenge of writing about the internment. The student examples and recommended readings that accompany each lesson offer different approaches prospective writers can take. The annotated bibliography at the end of the book contains reference information and short descriptions of the recommended readings and other resources.

Our hope is that this book will encourage other communities to begin their own writing groups. We also encourage those who do not have the benefit of a community to explore their own voice. The legacy of the writers in this collection is to inspire and to invite each of us to discover our own truths to share.

— Jill Mari Shiraki, Director of Programs
Japanese Cultural & Community Center of Northern California

[1] From its humble beginnings at South Park in the late 1800s, San Francisco's Japantown was displaced due to the Great Fire & Earthquake in 1906, forcibly removed to the Tanforan Assembly Center in 1942, and redefined as part of the Redevelopment Agency plans from 1956 to 1980.

Acknowledgments

For the courage and willingness to share their memories, discover their voices, and delve into the camp experience, we at the Japanese Cultural & Community Center of Northern California (JCCCNC) would like to thank all of the writers of the Internment Autobiography Writing Workshop. The contributing authors are: Florence Dobashi, Kiku Funabiki, Sato Hashizume, Fumi Hayashi, Florence Nakamura, Ruth Okimoto, Wayne Osaki, Toru Saito, Daisy Satoda, Harumi Serata, and Michi Tashiro. During production, they gave helpful comments and critiques of various sections of the book, as well as other useful information and resources.

Ensconced in the Nichiren Buddhist Church in San Francisco, Brian Komei Dempster, a talented Sansei writer, appeared at the JCCCNC one day and offered to facilitate writing workshops. What has transpired is no accident. Brian has patiently guided our way with his insights, gentle nudging, and skillful techniques, which allowed the writers' stories to unfold. We thank him as our instructor, editor, and dear friend.

For their direction and assistance, we thank our publishing team at Kearny Street Workshop: Nancy Hom and Claire Light. We extend a very special thank you to our designer Zand Gee—her delicate touch and sharp eye made the publishing process magical. For capturing life "from our side of the fence" in their art, we are grateful to Ruth Y. Okimoto for the cover drawing, Kimi Kodani Hill for permission to use the Chiura Obata artwork, and Naoko Yoshimura Ito for the quilt design.

The work on this book was made much easier by the support and guidance of others. We are indebted to Patricia Wakida of Heyday Books for her experience and insight. The following individuals provided excellent feedback on the project: Sabina Chen, Edmond Chow, Jay Ruben Dayrit, Stuart and Renko Dempster, Lillian Howan, Roy Kamada, Anastasia Royal, and Steven Salchak. And to others who helped in editorial and project-related decisions, but are too numerous to name here, our grateful thanks.

We are honored to have received funding from the California Civil

Liberties Public Education Program (CCLPEP). We thank Dr. Kevin Starr, State Librarian, Diane Matsuda, Program Director, and the staff at the California State Library for their assistance. We would also like to acknowledge Assemblyman Michael Honda of San Jose who initiated the California Civil Liberties Public Education Act in the California State Assembly in 1998. Our appreciation goes out to the Advisory Committee of the CCLPEP that backs the efforts of so many grantee projects. In addition, we gratefully acknowledge the Zellerbach Family Fund, which believed in the potential of our project early on and continues to support community arts. And a special thank you to Union Bank of California and the California Bank and Trust whose contributions assist us with the marketing and outreach of this book.

We extend warm thanks to Executive Director Paul Osaki and the staff at the JCCCNC who offers us a home away from home. We thank the Senior Women Writers at the JCCCNC who emanate warmth and laughter. They, like the Internment Autobiography Writing Workshop, share the struggle to tell their stories.

Our editor, Brian Komei Dempster is indebted to the Ishida family for allowing him to live as a caretaker at the Nichiren Buddhist Church of America, where he completed much of his work on this project. He is also grateful to both the Ragdale Foundation and the Ucross Foundation for residency fellowships, which gave him additional time and space. A special thank you to Garrett Hongo for his wisdom and friendship. Finally, Brian wishes to thank his parents, Stuart and Renko, his brother, Loren, and his wife, Grace, for their continued love and support.

On behalf of the writers and production team, we thank our spouses, family and friends whose support and constancy encourages us to share our voice with the community. — *J.M.S.*

A Note to the Reader

While the pieces in this anthology stand on their own, we have made a conscious effort to create a cultural and historical context for the reader. Within the pieces themselves, almost all Japanese words and phrases are italicized and are usually followed by their accompanying English definition in parentheses. In most cases where the author uses a Japanese word or phrase and does not translate it, the glossary near the end of the book gives the English version. In addition, we have provided definitions for the different Japanese generational terms that appear throughout the book, such as Issei, Nisei, and Sansei. A list of important historical references round out the glossary, followed by a table with significant information about the ten concentration camps where the authors were incarcerated during World War II. At times students refer to a camp by the city in which it is located, rather than by its official name. For example, the Central Utah War Relocation Center is commonly known as "Topaz." In addition, subdivisions are sometimes used (such as "Poston I") to indicate different sections within a particular concentration camp.

Throughout this project, we realized the value of reexamining the language we use to speak or write about the internment. For example, several students shared their experiences of working as docents for "America's Concentration Camps: Remembering the Japanese American Experience" curated by the Japanese American National Museum and presented at the California Historical Society. They spoke of how disturbing it was to realize that they had been conditioned to accept the American government's euphemisms for the incarceration experience, such as "assembly center" for "temporary detention center" and "relocation center" for "concentration camp." For the students, this realization was empowering. By choosing to use language that was more accurate to their experience, the students found more freedom to express in their writings what had really happened to them.

For photograph captions, we have replaced the euphemism "evacuee" with "internee" (which refers to Japanese Americans forcibly removed from their homes and imprisoned in a temporary detention center or concentration camp). In the glossary, "concentration camps" refers to the War Relocation Authority camps where the students were imprisoned, and "internment camps" refers to the Department of Justice camps. Terms such as "incarceration" and "internment" are used synonymously —instead of the euphemism "relocation"—to describe the camp experience as a whole. When the writers do use the government's wording, it designates the proper name of a specific place such as Tanforan Assembly Center or Minidoka War Relocation Center.

Though it is beyond the scope of this piece to provide a full scale discussion of euphemistic terminology, it is important to note that many authors, including Roger Daniels and Michi Weglyn, have used the term "concentration camps" in their books. Among the scholars who have written powerful commentaries about the issue of language are James Hirabayashi, Karen L. Ishizuka, Brian Niiya, and Raymond Okamura. Organizations such as the Japanese American National Museum in Los Angeles, where Ishizuka is Senior Curator, have had extensive dialogue with Japanese American and Jewish American leaders and scholars to pave the way to use "concentration camps" and other such words in exhibits like the one at the California Historical Society. Like them, we believe that language should be a conscious and informed choice, borne out of the knowledge that even a single word can have profound consequences.

Introduction

In January of 1999, a group of my Japanese American senior women writing students approached me in the lobby of the Japanese Cultural & Community Center of Northern California. "We want to write our internment stories," they stated adamantly. "We want our children and grandchildren to know what happened to us during World War II. Will you help us?"

I thought of my students and how they, like my then infant mother and her brothers and sisters, had experienced a significant part of their childhood and adolescence behind a barbed wire fence, often separated from other family members. Reflecting upon their request, I considered certain assumptions I had held over the years, assumptions only confirmed by what I had read about internment. Were Japanese Americans unwilling to speak about the war? Was their silence a result of passivity or fear or repression? Were those who did speak an exception to the rule?

My students wanted to break their silences through writing, but had not yet found a vehicle to do so. If I could structure a way for them to document their memories, then perhaps together we could preserve the legacy of the camps and, at the same time, pay homage to other Japanese American internees—those living who were not yet ready or able to articulate their stories and those who had died before they had the chance to do so. My students were entrusting me with something I was not sure could be handled: the subject of incarceration was a glowing coal I wanted both to hold and let go. How could I help them write about these momentous events? How could I help them capture memories I had not personally experienced? How could I help them with the inevitable pain and emotion that would come up as they sifted through the past?

Despite these concerns, I welcomed the challenges of this unique opportunity. The prospect of being chosen as a guide for them excited me and resonated with my own journey to uncover my family's past in San Francisco's Japantown. As a caretaker of my deceased grandfather's church—the Nichiren Buddhist Church of America—I discovered that the building had been leased out to tenants while he and his family were incarcerated. When the family returned after their release from camp, they found the church desecrated: the wallpaper was peeling, the attic looted, the scuffed floor sprinkled with shards of vases. As they swept the floor and pasted back the wallpaper, once again they made the church into a home. If I too had returned to my grandfather's church to continue preserving and healing it, then a part of my journey was to help document the stories of the community of which he had been an integral part.

Keeping these stories alive in the community is crucial. I did not learn of America's concentration camps until 1988—as an eighteen-year-old undergraduate at the University of Washington—in an introductory Asian American Studies course taught by Professor Peter Bacho. The class text, *Prejudice, War, and the Constitution*, gave a step-by-step analysis of the decision by the United States government to incarcerate 120,000 Japanese Americans during the Second World War on the basis of "military necessity."

    "Is it true?" I asked my mother.

    "What?"

    "That our family was put in camps during the war?"

    "Yes. But I remember little."

I tried to stitch together her hazy memories with details I drew out from the other members of the family who were willing to speak. Weaving together these various accounts, I developed a series of poems based on my family's life in the camps. Along the way I discovered such poignant and moving poems as "Stepchild" and "Something Whispered in the *Shakuhachi*" from Garrett Hongo's *Yellow Light*. I discovered *After We Lost Our Way*, a volume of poetry in which David Mura characterizes and examines the legacy of internment passed down to him and connects it to other historical atrocities. Hongo and Mura wrote powerful narratives about the internment and yet, like me, had not actually been internees. As an aspiring young poet, this tradition empowered me, providing models to which I could apprentice myself. In the examples of Hongo and Mura, I found literary strategies and approaches through which I could articulate both the silences my ancestors held and the stories they revealed to me.

While I was frustrated that my mother and her family had not volunteered their experience of the camps, talking to me about it only when I asked, I could understand their pain, their hesitation. More than anything, I was filled with a rage, an anger sparked by the fact that I had been blindsided by a history from which I had been unknowingly cut off. This anger was directed at the American government and their every attempt to remove this history from the public conscience; at every American history class that failed even to mention the existence of the camps; at every American history textbook that was guilty, by omission, of erasing the internment from its pages.

From Our Side of the Fence contains the selected writings of eleven (nine female, two male) former internees, the majority of whom are Nisei, second-generation Japanese Americans. These authors work primarily in the form of memoir—first-person prose and poetry rooted in personal experience. They humanize the facts of their incarceration and its ongoing impact on their lives. They give voice to a history that has been silenced by American institutions and that has been kept silent, in particular by their parents, who rarely spoke about the internment.

This collection shows that, through language, what has been suppressed can be recorded. Only through the courage to speak can some measure of justice be achieved. Indeed, it is only through documentation—like the testimonies of former detainees at hearings held by the

U.S. Commission on Wartime Relocation and Internment of Civilians—that every surviving Japanese American internee received a presidential apology along with a redress check for $20,000 each.

This anthology not only bears witness to the power of the word, but underscores the healing ability of the creative process through which silence can be broken. In class, certain students were hesitant to write. Because none of them were professional writers, they tended to underestimate their talent and the power of their life experiences. Once they began freewriting, however, they discovered a wealth of material which had been lying dormant, waiting to be excavated. And as they began these excavations, they found that the act of writing was a cumulative process in which the completion of one piece generated new ideas and inspiration for the next.

While *From Our Side of the Fence* includes many writings that began as freewrites, all of them required revision. Students were initially surprised by the amount of praise and criticism I penned in the margins of their papers, but they grew accustomed to the process of receiving and responding to constructive criticism. In our work together, I became a clearer, more efficient editor, and the students learned how to effectively process my feedback.

These finished products are the result of much labor and thought. They have the imprint of each writer's voice, its individual pitch and timbre. They are ordered chronologically so that you, the reader, are able to trace each writer's geographical and psychological journey through the war. By reading these authors as a group, you can examine how each responded to similar circumstances and the extent to which their perceptions of America forever changed as a result of their imprisonment.

If you are someone who has never much thought about or perhaps even heard of the internment, my students and I hope this book makes you want to learn more. If you are a professor, we hope it will find a home in your libraries and in your classrooms. If you are a schoolteacher, we encourage you to use this book as a tool to educate your students about the emotional and psychological impact of internment upon youth and how these experiences relate to present-day issues of racism and cultural diversity. If you are a student, we want this book to bring you the personal stories of the internment; we hope it inspires you to research your own family history and to write it down.

If you are a Holocaust survivor or descendant, may this book add to the continuing dialogue between our communities about the camp experience of the Jewish people in Europe and the Japanese Americans in the United States.

If you are a former internee who wants to chronicle your wartime memories, we invite you to do so by following the lesson plans near the end of the book. If you are a group who wants to begin your own Internment Autobiography Writing Workshop, we suggest you use this book as both a workshop model and a curriculum guide. If you are an Issei or Nisei, we strongly urge you to record your story in order to preserve our country's history so that Sansei, Yonsei, and others will know the legacy of internment. If you have not yet spoken, we hope that this book helps you turn your silence into words.

— Brian Komei Dempster,
San Francisco, California

To Allison —
With pleasure in our meeting
and with blessings for your support.

About the Editor

Brian Komei Dempster is a Sansei whose mother's family was interned at Topaz concentration camp in Utah and Crystal City internment camp in Texas. He completed B.A. degrees in American Ethnic Studies and English at the University of Washington, graduating Phi Beta Kappa. As a Rackham Merit Fellow, he attended the University of Michigan where he received his M.F.A. in Creative Writing. He is the recipient of a Creative Artist Grant from the Arts Foundation of Michigan and the Michigan Council for Arts and Cultural Affairs, and he has been awarded residency fellowships to the Ragdale Foundation, Vermont Studio Center, Villa Montalvo, and Ucross Foundation. His poems have appeared in The Asian Pacific American Journal, Crab Orchard Review, Green Mountains Review, Ploughshares, *and* Quarterly West. *Currently he resides in San Francisco in the church founded by his grandfather, a Buddhist priest. He divides his time between caretaking for his ancestral home, teaching, and completing his first collection of poems.*

Brian Komei Dempster
Seattle, WA
September 10, 2004

Anthology

❧

Florence Ohmura Dobashi

Kiku Hori Funabiki

Sato Hashizume

Fumi Manabe Hayashi

Florence Miho Nakamura

Ruth Y. Okimoto

Yoshito Wayne Osaki

Toru Saito

Daisy Uyeda Satoda

Harumi Serata

Michi Tashiro

OPPOSITE: Chiura Obata, "Regulations," 1943. Watercolor on paper, 18 x 12.5 in. Courtesy of the Obata family.

Florence Ohmura Dobashi

❧

After Pearl Harbor

At about one o'clock we heard a car door slam outside, and a boy rushed into our home. "Japan has bombed Pearl Harbor," he exclaimed. "They've declared war on the United States!" At first we thought he was joking, but we turned on the radio and heard the news. I believe that I was never so shocked in all my life. On the night of December 5th, 1941, our eighth and ninth grade party had taken place. We had played hilarious games, had fun, and shared warm camaraderie. On Sunday morning, the 7th, I had attended Sunday School as usual. Immediately after the adult worship service, I had stayed home, but the rest of my family had gone to Los Angeles to attend the wedding and reception of a former Riverside girl. Since I was home alone, two of my friends—twin sisters, Mary and Martha—had come over for the afternoon after we had lunch at their home. And now the boy warned, "Some drunkards are threatening to kill all the Japanese they can find—so be careful!"

After he left we locked all the doors and hoped for the best. Then I thought of my family in Los Angeles, and fear crept into my mind. "Suppose they should be hurt in some way?" I thought. After dinner at the twins' house, they walked me home, and I was all alone that evening. I sat hunched over in front of the radio, anxiously listening to news reports, and wishing that my family would come home soon. They finally returned safely late that night.

The next morning when I started out for school, I wondered how my friends would treat me now. To my relief, the only time anyone

ABOVE: Florence Ohmura Dobashi, 1945 and 2001.
OPPOSITE: Headlines of newspapers in the San Francisco Bay Area presaged on February 27, 1942, the forced removal of persons of Japanese ancestry from military areas. Dorothea Lange, WRA photograph, National Archives at College Park.

mentioned the bombing to me was when a girl asked, "What do you think of the war?" I was so surprised that all I said was, "Oh, I don't know exactly." She and I just laughed it off, and I was put at ease. Otherwise, everyone was just the same as ever. In fact, some acquaintances went out of their way to greet me and seemed even friendlier than before, and I continued with my activities at school.

Mr. Crane, the principal, held a special school assembly that morning where he discussed the previous day's events and reminded everybody, "The Japanese Americans (JAs) are not responsible for the war. They are Americans." In those days Riverside was a quiet town of about 60,000 people with perhaps a couple hundred JAs. My junior high school of about 1,000 students had only five JAs, one "Negro"; the rest were Caucasians. Race or ethnicity didn't seem to matter to the students, I thought. I had held many class offices and been elected to the Student Body Council, following in the footsteps of another JA girl a year ahead of me.

Nevertheless, I wished that my family and I didn't have the same appearance as the enemy, and I feared that we might be mistaken as such by strangers. We heard stories from friends in Los Angeles about Japanese Americans who were taunted with racial epithets and suffered physical assaults.

After school one day, I walked home and saw my father in the back-yard, burning stacks of documents in a trash can. I was horrified but also amused, because we were in full view of the *hakujin* (Caucasian) neighbors across the street and whoever else happened to walk or drive by. "I'm destroying the records of the local Japanese Association," Pop explained. "You see, I'm the Secretary, and I don't want the authorities to know who the members are. The FBI thinks the Japanese Associations are pro-Japan even though they aren't. In other towns they're putting members in prison. I expect they'll pick me up whether or not I burn these papers. As the minister of the Japanese Congregational Church, I'm a community leader."

Late at night on February 27, 1942, the FBI did come to get Pop. There were four male agents—all tall and intimidating. They trashed Pop's study, pulled books off the shelves, and scattered them on the floor. They slid open his file cabinets and desk drawers and shuffled through his papers, throwing them sheet by sheet to the floor. They poked into dressers, closets and the rest of the house, looking for anything that might incriminate him. One agent searched Pop's closet. "Here's something, a weapon!" he exclaimed and held it up to show to the others. It was Pop's samurai sword, an heirloom that he had brought from Japan as a keepsake when he came to America at the age of 18 in February

1907. "It's contraband," another agent said. Then they took away my father, along with his sword, a spot-flashlight (used to spotlight performers in Sunday School pageants), and some other items.

After my father was gone I recalled the beliefs of *Obasan* (Auntie), who unfortunately had gone to Japan with her husband and daughter in April 1941. "The Japanese people are superior to everybody else," she had always maintained. Although I didn't agree with her super-race notion, maybe her endless repetition of this statement throughout my childhood made me proud of being Japanese. Still, after Pearl Harbor and even more so after my father was taken away, I wished that we were not Japanese.

As the so-called evacuation day approached Mr. Crane said, "I'm sorry you have to leave. We'll miss you." Many school friends expressed similar sentiments. Some of them said, "We can't understand why you have to leave your homes and go into camps without a trial or something like that." Regardless of how any of us felt, I knew I'd be treated differently by the government and could not prevent our being sent away. Neither could my family, the principal, or my friends. I was confused, a jumble of mixed feelings.

The Blanket

One day in 1942, when I was 14 years old, my girlfriend Dorothy told me, "My stepmother is sleeping with my brother. I can hear them because our beds are separated only by blankets hung on ropes strung from wall to wall." Dorothy continued angrily, "She seems to have some sort of hold over Don—or is it true love?" I was surprised and didn't know what to say. Don, who was in his 20s, later joined the army and never came home. He wasn't killed. He stayed in France and married a French woman. I think he might have done this to escape the clutches of their stepmother. Since I lost contact with Dorothy years ago, I don't know whether Don ever returned to America.

On many hot summer evenings in "Roastin' Poston,"[1] I hung out with our neighbors, Judy and her older brother, Jeff, in their "front yard." Other young men who were Jeff's age often came over to visit. One, in particular, always flirted with Judy and she with him. She used to say plaintively, "At sweet sixteen I should be having fun dating boys my own age. Instead, here I am, pining away for Mack." Judy and I thought he was an "older man," but, in reality, he was only about 19 years old. Sometimes Judy and Mack would lie on a table in the yard, completely covered by a blanket, and I would naively ask, "Why are they under the blanket when it's so hot?" As the blanket undulated, I added, "What are they doing?" The answer always was, "Oh, you're so green, so 'yongu.' "[2] I'd say, "Why won't you tell me?" They'd roll their eyes and reply, "Cuz you're just a kid. But you'll know someday." Sure enough, I do.

[1] *We often referred to our camp as "Roastin 'Poston" half jokingly and half bitterly.*
[2] *Camp-style broken English for "young."*

The Loyalty Questionnaire

After we'd been incarcerated for nearly a year, government officials finally decided to determine who was "disloyal" and who was "loyal." They devised a dubious questionnaire that everybody of age 17 and above was required to answer. Later, in mid-1944 when I was 16 years old, arrangements were made for me to finish high school in a suburb of Cleveland, Ohio. In order to leave camp I was required to answer affirmative to the infamous loyalty questions #27 and #28. The malicious intent of these questions completely contradicted the kind sentiments I had received from those I'd known at school in Riverside. The principal and my non-JA friends could not prevent this ultimate insult.

Regarding #27, which required bearing arms in defense of the country or joining the Women's Army Auxiliary Corps, my reaction was, "What nerve they have to ask us such a question after putting us into camps just because we look Japanese!" When actually faced with the need to answer the question, I also thought, "What? Me? I'm only 16 years old. They shouldn't be telling me to answer this. Can't the government do anything according to its own rules?"

Regarding #28, I resented being asked to forswear allegiance to the Emperor of Japan because I could not forswear an allegiance I never had. It was like being asked, "Have you stopped beating your wife?" The question itself implied guilt.

Florence Ohmura Dobashi's "Citizen's Indefinite Leave" card. She states: "In order to obtain leave clearance and this green card, we inmates had to answer YES to both questions #27 and #28."

If I had not wanted to leave camp, I might have answered "No" to both #27 and #28. However, I chose to be practical and said "Yes." Otherwise I would have had to stay in camp for the duration of the war, sacrifice my chance to experience life in the Midwest, and possibly jeopardize my future education. It seemed foolhardy to make those sacrifices and feel like a lonely martyr, yet I was bothered by not answering honestly. Still, I am consoled because thousands of other people who left camps during that period also had to answer "Yes-Yes" regardless of their real sentiments or convictions. It was the only way out.

❧

Racism and Silence

Although my academic score was the second highest in the senior class at Brecksville High School, a month before graduation I was told that the third highest student would be the salutatorian. The teacher explained, "Your voice is too soft to be heard in the auditorium." But since the school did have a public address system, I wondered if the faculty's decision was made because they didn't want to honor a "Jap," a person who looked like the enemy. I should have told the teacher that, in junior high school, I was on the Student Body Council whose members took turns presiding over the weekly assembly. I should have told her I had spoken several times without any complaint, even from the far reaches of the balcony, and my junior high's auditorium was three times larger than Brecksville High's. I should have been assertive and asked to be allowed to try out. However, with my parents 2,000 miles away in the Poston concentration camp and no adult available to intercede on my behalf, I thought I had no choice and complied silently.

In our graduation ceremony the graduating seniors were to walk down the aisle to the front of the auditorium in couples. Girls and boys were matched according to height; the shortest girl was paired with the shortest boy and so on. Martin T. and I were the shortest in the class. Jim, who was slightly taller than Martin, came to my home a few days before graduation. He announced, "I'm going to escort you for the ceremony because Martin doesn't want to walk with a 'Jap.' " Jim probably thought he was doing me a favor, but I thought I would have been better off not knowing about Martin's insult. I thought Jim wanted me to admire his noble willingness to walk with a "Jap" because after he told me, he kissed me. I was shocked and recoiled. Jim could have been kind—if he had simply said that he wanted to escort me, I would have been blissfully unaware of any slight. Then I might have reacted differently when he made his overture. I had already been robbed of the salutatory title and speech. Now Martin's remark and Jim's subtly racist behavior completely spoiled what had been a pleasant year and what should have been a joyous occasion. Again, I was silent.

I never told my parents about these incidents so I was surprised, after I returned home to Riverside in October 1945, when my mother mentioned that they had heard about the salutatorian matter from an Issei minister who was a family friend. He had been living in Cleveland at the time and had been looking after me without my knowledge. I dimly recall that he was at the graduation ceremony and that he greeted me with a handshake and smile. I'm glad he told my folks. Otherwise, my parents would not have been able to tell me, "We're proud of how well you did in school. Even though you were not publicly honored, we know that you deserved the recognition." Without their comforting words, I might have continued to suffer in silence.

Some fifty years later, this is not a pleasant incident to reminisce about. However, it has come to mind occasionally as I have sat down again in other auditoriums and seen each valedictorian and salutatorian, and heard the same claps and cheers, not for me, but for someone else. I'm happy for them. Deep down though, it still annoys and irritates me that I couldn't include "salutatorian" as an honor on my résumé.

❦

Apple Butter

In our mess hall we were never served butter or margarine. We heard that it was not available because of the war effort, but I never understood what the war had to do with our lack of butter. And later, when I found out certain foods were rationed during the war, I wondered whether our allotments of butter or margarine were being stolen and sold on the black market. We were given a substitute called "apple butter" to use on bread, rolls, and other food. Despite its name, it bore no resemblance to butter. It was a dark brown substance with the texture and flavor of unsweetened applesauce. It did nothing to make the bread products taste better. I used to think, "Day after day, year after year, no real butter." I hated it. When I left camp in 1944, I was able to forget apple butter because I never saw or heard of it again.

Fifty-three years later, a young Japanese American friend named Ann invited me to dinner at her home. She served sourdough bread but didn't provide any butter or margarine. Thinking she had simply forgotten it, I asked if she had some. Ann replied, "I don't have any because I'm on a low-fat diet." Instead she offered me, of all things, apple butter. My eyes widened in astonishment, and I burst into laughter so hard that my eyes started to water.

As I reached the point of tears, I blurted out, "I thought apple butter was concocted by the government to make us inmates of the concentration camps more miserable." My outburst was met with an awkward silence. Attempting to break the tension, I said, "I didn't know it was available in grocery stores and much less that anybody would buy it." Ann and her other guests, all Japanese Americans younger than I, said they had never experienced the so-called Relocation Centers. They didn't seem to understand or appreciate the irony of my laughter. Ann asked naively, "Do you want it?" and placed it on the table even though I grimaced and shook my head. During the rest of the meal I avoided looking at the jar but couldn't stop the recollection of dreary mess hall food and dreaded apple butter. This is when and how I finally learned that apple butter really was not a diabolical creation made by the people who put us into the camps.

Florence Ohmura Dobashi

Florence Ohmura Dobashi, born and raised in Southern California, was interned at the Colorado River Relocation Center in Unit I (Poston I) near Parker, Arizona, at the age of fourteen in 1942. She later attended the University of California (UC) Berkeley as a Public Health major and graduated from UC Los Angeles with a B.A. from the Political Science Department in International Relations with an emphasis on the Far East.

Fresh out of school, she thought that social and political conditions throughout the world were deplorable and wanted to try to help improve them. Aware of the unpopular wartime stand taken by the Northern California Branch of the American Civil Liberties Union (ACLU) in opposition to the mass removal and detention of Japanese Americans, she applied for an opening and eventually went to work there. At the time, she and Ernest Besig, the director, comprised its entire staff. After six years of assisting in legal cases and participating in the organization's growth, she moved to a part-time job with the ACLU's General Counsel, Wayne M. Collins, for another two years. During this period, the 1950s, she was active in and served on the boards of the Young Democrats Club, Japanese American Citizens League, Buchanan Street YMCA, and various local Nikkei political groups.

Later, she worked for the UC San Francisco medical school, where her public health, political, and business background proved to be useful. She retired as an administrative analyst after twenty years. She now enjoys various activities, including the Internment Autobiography Writing Workshop, which has helped her to articulate her experiences and to learn about those of other individuals.

Kiku Hori Funabiki

The Gap

The "Night to Remember" happened at a dance in a recreation hall on my block. My teenage shyness rendered me tongue-tied, a wallflower. Boys liked girls who did all the talking, since many of them were as shy as me. I was a late bloomer, but in my slow development, my fantasies were rich. They ran the gamut from innocent flirtations with a golden prince to a wild date with a cute, loud, hang-it-out *yogore* (punk).

The evening went uneventfully until the last dance when the lights were turned out. The music was always Glenn Miller's "Moonlight Serenade." Miller's sweet melody, which the DJs played over and over, sent the couples into a romantic bliss. It was sway and smooch time.

Suddenly, the entrance door flung open, hitting the wall with a crash. The lights flashed on, cutting through the blackness like swords. The entrance of Mr. Sato, block moralist, was as daunting as that of Mifune, the maverick samurai. Sato-san screamed in his earthy Japanese, "*Yura nani shiyoru ka* (What the hell do you guys think you're doing)?" Mr. Sato probably had expected to catch us in a wild orgy.

A roomful of teenagers squinted from the cruel flash of light . . . boys with lipstick smears on their acned faces, girls who wore their hair in perfect pompadours, now undone, stood stunned as their romantic bliss was mercilessly shot down. "*Mo hayo kaire* (Now hurry up and get on home)!" Sato-san barked his order even louder. We gathered our cloaks and slinked out as if we had been dashed with ice water. It was a generational showdown, and the lone elder stood his ground this time.

Sato-san wasted no time the following morning. At breakfast, in the mess hall, he continued the moralistic haranguing to a captive audience

ABOVE: Kiku Hori Funabiki, 1943 and 2001.
OPPOSITE: Kiku (left), age 2, with her neighbor, "Teddy," Los Angeles, California, 1926.

of mainly Issei. A fundamentalist Christian, he was relishing the Bible-thumping preacher role from his bully pulpit, warning the elders how camp life and episodes like the Rec. Hall Raid of the night before spelled doom for the youth. They were becoming deranged and incorrigible sinners.

As the word spread throughout the camp, titters were heard from all young adults, some gathering in clusters to share the story of the Rec. Hall Raid. But the elders were not amused. I'm sure church attendance was up that Sunday for the Issei to pray for redemption of the misguided youth.

To us teenagers, this generational confrontation was normal, amusing, and just the comic relief we all needed from a world war raging beyond the barbed wire.

Japanese American National Museum's 1997 Calendar – May. Kiku states: "From the images of the '40s—turntables, 78s, dance bids—a treasury of sweet memories began to surface like bubbles. These were universal symbols of teenage life even within barbed wire compounds. We were a subculture constituting the largest age group in camp. Restrictions placed upon us, such as curfews and loss of privacy, did not prevent us from seeking fun."

❦

Return, But Not to My Backyard
(an excerpt)

With the "Evacuation Orders" we were removed from a beautiful home that Papa had built only twelve years before. We entrusted the house to our bank which assured us that they would screen for applicants who would be responsible tenants. However, they let us down. The irresponsible occupants—shipyard workers who had migrated in throngs from the Midwest and South—lodged there in shifts around the clock, turning the handsome structure into a "flophouse." The entire interior was in shambles: garbage was strewn on the floors; electrical fixtures were left broken; rodents were running free; and cobwebs hung from the ceilings.

We could not gain occupancy for about a year during the eviction process. Papa, Mama, and I stayed in a Seventh Day Adventist Hostel in a room half the size of our unit in camp. I attended classes at U.C. Berkeley during the day and worked on the house with Papa at night.

The renovation took almost a year. Although my older brother took a leave from his work in New York to help settle us into our house and to start the renovation process, he was called back to a demanding job and to his family, which included his first-born son. My other brother was finishing up his last year at a college on the East Coast. Mama had been weakened by a minor stroke she had suffered in camp. The Herculean task of renovation was left to Papa and me. In order to make the house liveable again, we had to fumigate, clear debris, strip paint with acid, scrape layers of dirt ground into the floors, and so on. Still, we were more fortunate than most returnees who were virtually homeless and stayed in makeshift shelters such as the gymnasium of the local Buddhist Church.

The hostile social climate when we returned was nothing that we had known when we left. Before the war I had never been ignored by store clerks, but after our return it was a common occurrence. I grew even more frustrated as I tried to engage the services of contractors who seemed to feel that we could be deferred indefinitely.

In the cities, racism was more subtle and insidious than the open hostility in rural areas. Returnees faced life-threatening situations. A friend informed me that on one occasion, she, with her family, had to dodge bullets from a drive-by shooting. Then she shared a story of a neighbor who had his house torched. We had no protection from these incidents. Decades later, at the Congressional hearing for Redress in

Washington, D.C., Committee members relentlessly used the rationale that we were sent to concentration camps as protection from the hostile element of American society who equated us with the enemy. Where was that protection during our return when we were actually in the cross-hairs?

What spared me from becoming consumed by resentment and bitterness was bearing witness to Papa's undaunting spirit to reclaim his life. After his FBI seizure in early 1942, Papa and 1,200 Issei men and some women were incarcerated in prisoner-of-war camps, and constantly moved to different sites for "security reasons." The only charge was that these men were Japanese and active in supporting their communities.

Three years after his release, Papa, now at retirement age, was forced to begin over again. It was back to 1902 when he disembarked in San Francisco as an immigrant to America with no shelter, no work, and meager funds. Still, with each adversity, he rose like the *Daruma*, symbol of determination and perseverance. How many stories of hardships and heartbreaks must there be of fellow ex-internees who had to rebuild their broken lives.

 Daruma: "Seven falls and eight rises" is a phrase associated with the Daruma; this papier-mâché doll is weighted on the bottom so it will always upright itself. Daruma owners hope for inner strength and determination and for the ability to rise eight times even though they fall down seven.

❧

Silence . . . No More

Silence, forty years of silence
Forty years of anger, pain, helplessness
Shackled in the hearts
Of Issei, Nisei, Kibei.

Many died in silence
Some by their own hands
Some by others.

Today
The survivors

Stood tall, strong, proud
And vowed
No more *enryo, giri, gaman.*

Today
The survivors
Cried out redress, restitution, reparations
Shattering the silence:

        for
a father detained in five
prisoner-of-war camps in America
for the "crime" of being Japanese
who joined his loved ones
in yet another barbed wire compound
then returned home to die at seventy-three
struggling to reclaim his life
in San Francisco; [1]

        for
a mother whose demons drove her
to hammer her infant to death
now skipping merrily after butterflies
in the snow;

        for
a brother, honor student,
star athlete, Purple Heart veteran
now alone in a sleazy Seattle hotel room
sitting on the edge of a cot
rocking, rocking;

        for
a girl of fourteen
mother to the Japanese American children
of Petersburg
orphaned by the FBI seizure
of all Japanese adults
still ashamed over the memory
of detouring the jailhouse,
when she caught sight of her father
waving desperately to her through steel bars;

                    for
        a baby whose whimpers
        were silenced forever
        in a camp hospital
        where the Caucasian doctor never came
        for her
        after his son was killed
        in the Pacific;

    Silence
    Silence, no more

            . . . no more.

[1] *Refers to author's father, Sojiro Hori.*

Note: This poem was written after the public hearings in 1982 held by the Commission on Wartime Relocation and Internment in ten cities. Many ex-detainees spoke out for the first time. The incidents are taken from actual testimonies given at the hearings in San Francisco and Seattle.

In 1984, I read this piece with my testimony at the Congressional hearing before a subcommittee of the House Judiciary Committee in Washington, D.C., and it was transcribed into the Congressional Records.

The Japanese American community was indeed silent no more. In 1991, the long, hard-fought battle for redress and reparations was won with the issuance of a presidential apology and a check for $20,000 to each of the survivors of the unjust, mass detention.

Games "Justice" Plays
(an excerpt)

It was no accident that the harshest questioning during the entire hearing was leveled at a petrified Asian female totally inexperienced in Constitutional matters, whom they perceived to be an easy target. My only experience in a courtroom had been to challenge a parking ticket. In contrast, the interrogation of the only other ex-detainee, a male, filled only two pages with innocuous questions. "Did you have to sell your property when you left? Were you allowed short leaves from camp?"

The Congressional Records show that the rambling, vague, and intimidating questioning of me by a sometimes misinformed Committee member goes on for seven pages. One of Congressman Thomas Kindness' (cruel joke?) questions rambles on for almost a full page. He is essentially trying to get me to concur that the measures the government took, specifically, our removal and illegal imprisonment in barbed wire compounds, were "for our protection." It was verbal stalking. I stood my ground with white-knuckle tenacity. Mr. Kindness was not going to have me buckle under his constant railing with the "protection" argument. It was a cat and mouse game.

The following statements are taken verbatim from the hearing and are entered in the Congressional Records:

> **Ms. Funabiki:** As you heard, German-Americans and Italian-Americans were not sent away. They were accorded equal protection under the law. We would have wanted to be protected by that same law.

> **Mr. Kindness:** Presumably your father was. If he was arrested by the FBI under the Enemy Aliens Act, he was entitled to a court hearing and so on. I would gather that he might have been targeted because of the business[2] he was in, which would be ideal for intelligence gathering, and even for espionage, I suppose, if one was theorizing about how this sort of thing is done. He had contact with a lot of people of Japanese ancestry or who may have come from Japan fairly recently and placing them in homes where intelligence could be gathered perhaps. I suppose that sort of thinking must have been involved in order for the arrest to be made.

I sat on the hot seat agonizing in a cold sweat for an hour and a half. During this time, the loud blast of a buzzer went off, signalling a mandatory floor appearance of all Congressmen to assemble immediately to the main chamber to cast their votes. This occurred twice during my presentation. The Congressman zeroed in with the final blow when he delivered the implication of "espionage," a flagrant charge of guilt by association. This was the final twist of the blade.

---

[2] *My father ran an employment agency for domestics who were placed in Caucasian homes.*

Note: My father and hundreds of Issei men were seized by the FBI after Pearl Harbor and incarcerated in POW camps for as long as three years. The charge was that they were Japanese and "dangerous enemy aliens." This painful memory of almost sixty years ago had been tucked away, but surfaced in full as I followed the Wen Ho Lee case which still has not been laid to rest. The interrogation of my father was not of the same intensity as that directed at Doctor Lee, but there is a clear parallel, that of guilt by association. My heart aches for the members of the Lee family who are still on an emotional bungee jump.

❦

Arthur

At John Swett Primary School in the inner city of San Francisco, three classes of third graders crowded snugly into one room. Some sat cross-legged on the floor, gathering around my feet. The majority of them were African Americans from the nearby housing project. They had expressed curiosity to their teachers about a whole community of Japanese Americans who had committed no crime, but were forced to leave their homes and were sent to far away prison camps during World War II.

We—of the speaker's group of the Curriculum Committee at the National Japanese American Historical Society—had spoken to students at middle schools, high schools, and universities. This was my first assignment to speak to children so young.

To these third graders, the significance of the Bill of Rights was a concept a little beyond their comprehension. I thought I might reach them by bringing in various large-sized photos of camp life from the Historical Society files. Through these images I would show how things we take for granted were suddenly not there for us (privacy for one, which had some relevance to their lives).

"Although the washrooms separated men and women," I stated, "the open toilets with no partitions between them faced each other." These high-spirited kids expressed their distaste openly with their "yechs" and cries of "GROSS!"

I then showed them a photo of the quarters of a family of four who lived in a room so small that the Army cots on which they slept were placed a mere two feet apart. There is a young man playing cards on his cot. I explained, "The internees did the best they could to have some privacy by hanging blankets between the cots." I suddenly felt a small tap on my knee. An African American boy in front of me leaned toward me

and discreetly whispered out of earshot of the teacher, "So how did they do it?"

It was all I could do to contain myself. Arthur will never know the enormous challenge to my composure he presented. He was a sweet-faced but street savvy kid, perhaps eight years old. I learned his name from a little black girl seated next to him. Typically third grade, she was almost a head taller than little Arthur. When he took his place she gave him a healthy, big-sisterly jab in the ribs and scolded, "Shut up Arthur, shut up." She was as streetwise as he was.

Arthur scrunched up his shoulders and cupped his mouth, looking half-pleased, half-embarrassed. I gave him a smile to assure him that his candid and earthy comment was "cool" with me and gave Arthur a high five. I think he understood then that I would not disclose his comment to the teacher.

On my way home, as I drove past the projects, I thought of my new pal. His living situation there was probably not much better than ours had been in our makeshift barracks. In fact, his dwelling was probably more congested and lacking in privacy than ours since project tenants tended to double up with extended families.

I still think of Arthur with fondness and concern. I hope that conditions in his life will allow him to leave the projects some day for a better world. Will he fall prey to the crime he is constantly exposed to? Does he have a loving support system to give him guidance so he can ward off temptations? Does he have a strong role model? I ponder.

Kiku Hori Funabiki

Kiku Hori Funabiki was born July 4, 1924, in Japantown, San Francisco, and lived there most of her life except for her three-year internment in Heart Mountain, Wyoming. Upon resettlement in the Bay Area she attended UC Berkeley, then worked for United Airlines until retirement. Kiku lives in San Francisco with her husband, Walter. They have one daughter, Chiyomi.

One of the high points of her life was to go eyeball to eyeball with the "white male establishment" of the House Judiciary Committee in Washington, D.C., to appeal for redress and reparations.

In her retirement she has enjoyed Brian Komei Dempster's Internment Autobiography Writing Workshop with a group of spirited, gifted, and sometimes raucous Nisei whom she finds stimulating and challenging. She is grateful to Brian for having created an environment of openness where she is encouraged to journey into the layers of her inner self. She is deeply influenced by Julia Cameron, poet, essayist, and journalist. She likes Cameron's idea that writing is a form of prayer and meditation which can connect us to a deeper level of inner guidance.

Her goals are to continue to search and grow, to connect, to give back some of the blessings of her life, and to be playful.

Sato Hashizume

The Red, White, and Blue Badge

Walking home from school, I savored the May trees and floral colors. Suddenly, two gangly teenagers blocked my path, demanding, "Are you a Jap?" I stammered, "N-no . . . no, I–I'm not a Jap, I'm Japanese."

One boy stooped down to pick up something, and I began to run. A stick struck my back. I ran faster. "You dirty yellow Jap, go back where you belong," the boys shouted. A stone brushed my hair, whizzed passed my left ear. Missiles kept coming until I was out of range, but I kept running and running until I turned right on Jefferson street where I paused to peer over my right shoulder. With my heart pounding and beads of sweat rolling down my face, I stumbled into the lobby of my apartment building.

While giving serious thought to my survival, I rushed out the back door, down three houses to Joyce Chan's house to play. As Joyce opened the screen door, a large red, white, and blue badge jumped out at me. With the stars and stripes of the flag, the button displayed the words, "I AM A LOYAL CHINESE." I quickly traded my ten cents worth of candies for the prize.

At our house, when school was open, the options were either go to school or be sick in bed, so it never occurred to me to tell Papa or my sister Kiyoko about the incident. The following afternoon, armed with my new identity, I tentatively walked past Lincoln High School. My tormenters were nowhere in sight. Another boy looked up and I pointed to my chest. He seemed uninterested. Now, confident about its protection, I walked down Broadway, past the Foster and Kleiser billboard with a bayonet-bearing Japanese soldier, a caricature with slanted eyes and protruding teeth. On the top of the poster were the words, "WIN THE

ABOVE: Sato Hashizume, 1949 and 2001.
OPPOSITE: Sato (circled), Sunday School, Minidoka Relocation Center, c. 1943.

WAR," and on the bottom, "KILL A JAP."

Triumphant, I pushed open the heavy oak door to announce my success. Kiyoko spoke first. "The government issued an order that we must leave. We have one week to get rid of everything. We have to find a home for Kitty, your cat." I wailed, "No, not Kitty . . . nooo . . . noooo." I ran to the piano room and buried my face in my arms. The red, white, and blue badge, now forgotten, lay on the linoleum floor.

❦

The Food

The room was huge, with more picnic tables than I had ever seen, and every table was filled with black-haired people like me. My brothers, George and Tom, joined their teenage buddies in the far corner of the room where I lost track of them, and my sisters, Kiyoko and Shigeko, sat with their friends three tables away. I was left at a table with Papa. This seating arrangement became permanent for the duration of our detention center stay. We never ate together as a family again.

I was used to home-cooked rice, miso soup, and pickled vegetables, so the army C rations from number 10 cans tested my stomach. I had never seen nor heard of hominy, big white kernels which looked like corn, but tasted bland and mealy. A frequent offering, it was served with slimy spinach or overcooked string beans, tinted greenish-black. The vegetables didn't resemble the fresh produce we ate at home, and Kiyoko questioned, "Do you think this food will make us sick?" I didn't touch the vegetables. When I was most hungry, I picked at the blanched weiners, grayish stews, and mushy corned beef hash.

One evening, we were served steak, a rare treat, but my excitement evaporated as I tried to cut the leathery meat with my limp, typhoid-vaccinated arm. My sisters insisted there was a conspiracy. "Every time we stand in the long lines for our typhoid shots, steak is served for supper," I overhead Shigeko say. "Then the steaks are thrown out because no one can cut them. I wonder who's behind this?"

Because special treats such as steak were difficult to enjoy, I was alert to a dinner-time announcement that claimed children would receive snacks. "When will we get the *oyatsu* (snacks)?" I pestered. "I wonder what they will give us? I hope they put some cupcakes or maybe a Babe Ruth in the bag." Kiyoko replied a bit wearily, "I doubt they'd have cupcakes. I'm going to pick up our package after lunch in the mess hall." I could hardly wait. My sweet tooth was ready.

She handed me a small box and two bags. "Here, you can open them," she said. Grabbing the bundle, I answered, "Oh boy, oh boy, I hope the stuff is good." I reached in the first bag and took out a dried apricot. As I put the tart fruit in my mouth, the sulfur smell made me grimace and spit it out. The other sack contained dried prunes. "That's all we need," Kiyoko moaned. "We've had the trots all week."

Not losing hope, I opened the plain grey box. "Graham crackers! There are graham crackers in here. I love graham crackers and milk." The crackers, attached in pairs, appeared pale beige and smooth. I ignored the off-color and texture, and I eagerly took a generous bite. The dry, flavorless biscuit crumbled into sawdust as I chewed. Close to tears, I complained, "What a cheat! These are awful; I can't eat this stuff. No one can. I bet the soldiers wouldn't eat it so they gave it to us."

When the mild spring days turned into a summer heat wave, I craved soft drinks. Cool places were nonexistent in the crowded compound, and people were frequently fainting. Adding to the oppressive hot weather, I had vaccination fevers and frequent diarrhea, both of which made me extremely thirsty. A small canteen opened near the arena. In exchange for a coupon, a drink could be purchased. "Do you have Hire's Root Beer?" I asked. The man behind the counter, answered,

ABOVE: Meals being served cafeteria-style, Manzanar War Relocation Center, California, 1942. Clem Albers, WRA photograph, National Archives at College Park.

"No, we carry only Dr Pepper and Orange Crush." I couldn't understand why they didn't have root beer when it tasted better than the other sodas. I settled for Orange Crush and drank what seemed like gallons, until I couldn't swallow one more mouthful. The orange soda, like the mess hall food, reminded me of what I lacked more than what I had. I imagined myself, sitting high on Doc Watson's chrome soda fountain stool, sipping a cool root beer, the foamy head sometimes topped with vanilla ice cream.

Indeed, root beer and graham crackers remained just a wistful dream since we were not allowed to go beyond the closely guarded encampment. We would have a special treat only if a non-internee worker or an outside friend brought it to us. Shigeko worked as a clerk in the administrative offices. When a non-interneee worker returned with her favorite Yaw's hamburger, popular among the young adults in Portland, she was ecstatic. "Guess what I ate today?" she teased. "I ate the juiciest, most perfectly cooked Yaw's hamburger. It was sooo delicious. I forgot how good it tasted. Yaw's special sauce was better than I remember and the juice dripped all over my hands. I had to use three napkins!" I tried to appear uninterested, but became green with envy when she bragged, "I don't have to eat mess hall food tonight."

The detention center, located in North Portland, was close enough for us to request a needed item or small treats from our long-time family friend, Mrs. Nelson. She visited us on her days off from the shipyards, loaded down with two shopping bags full of cheese and cracker snacks, peanut butter, and oreo cookies. She rode three buses and walked several blocks to reach the center at the town's outskirts. On one particular visit I spied a basket of glistening strawberries in one of the grocery bags. My mouth watered.

Kiyoko carefully parcelled the red jewels to each member of our family. We inhaled the sweet, tangy fragance and ate small bites to tantalize our tastebuds and make the moment last. "Yumm, oooh, aaah," we kept saying until no trace of the strawberries was left.

After we enjoyed the fruit, Kiyoko told Mrs. Nelson about her two-hour wait for a concrete tub to wash clothes. Mrs. Nelson shook her head, saying, "I don't understand why you are in here." When we told her that we would soon be moved to Idaho, she began to weep. Through her tears, she asked, "Why are they doing this to you? You are American citizens, born right here in Portland. It's wrong, all wrong. What is going to happen to you?"

We sat silently. We had no answers, only the memory of strawberries red and unreachable.

The Outhouse

I never had used it before. I wondered where the handle was to flush the toilet.

Without fail, I always kicked the front board twice. "Scorpions and black widow spiders hide in dark corners," my sisters warned. "Those insects can kill you if they sting or bite, so watch out! Always kick the toilet twice to knock them off before you sit down."

Since I wasn't sure my kicks were strong enough to dislodge the dangerous critters, I often added one or two more. As an added measure of safety, I never sat down.

At night, with decreased visibility, I needed forethought and nimbleness to maneuver my way to it. Using the flashlight, I located the two toilet openings, then balanced the flashlight towards the back of the bench where it would provide adequate light but not roll into one of the openings. My clothes came next. Finally, as always, I kicked the toilet twice.

One winter's night, the full moon illuminated the snow, and the icicles glistened from the barracks' roofs. Even the outhouse appeared serene in this picture postcard scene. The vapor from my breath and the snow crunching under my shoes reminded me of sled rides and snowball fights back in Portland.

Inside the unheated outhouse, snow dusted the seat and the floor. Fortified with a heavy coat and mittens, I fumbled with the flashlight and my clothes, but remembered to kick the toilet twice. Quickly completing my task, I pulled on my clothes. *WHAM!* With a heart-stopping jolt, ice crystals hit my skin. Shattering the stillness, I yelped, "YIIIIPES! OOOOH NOOOO!" I froze, rigid as an icicle, then shivered uncontrollably. I fled to the warmth of my potbellied stove.

Spring couldn't arrive fast enough. The indoor plumbing was completed in the women's rest rooms. I didn't have to kick the toilet anymore.

The Announcements

A hush swept over the mess hall. Mr. Funatake, the block manager, took his place in front with a folded paper in his hand. "I wonder who it is this time?" Shigeko whispered to Kiyoko. Mr. Funatake cleared his throat, then soberly read, "Sergeant Kenji Ono and Private 1st class John Otaki were killed in action in Italy on November 8th, 1944. Let's honor their bravery with a moment of silence."

I could hear Shigeko catch her breath. "Did he say Kenji Ono? Kenji was in my class. He was so smart and nice to everyone. I feel sorry for his mother. He's the only boy in the family, and they all looked up to him." Kiyoko spoke almost inaudibly. "Well, I know John's wife, she's in Chicago. She just had a baby." We left our food on the plates and bussed the dishes.

For the past four days, Mr. Funatake had announced the name of at least one deceased soldier at supper. I felt my stomach knot when he stood up with the paper in his hand. All of the men were from the greater Portland area, and we knew them. After a week, whenever Mr. Funatake got up to speak, I left the mess hall.

ABOVE: Honor roll at Minidoka. WRA photograph, National Archives at College Park.

Reminders of the fallen soldiers soon spread to the barracks. The Nambas created a shrine with a photograph of their uniformed son, his medals, and a carefully folded American flag. Others added incense and their copy of the well-read official letter. When Kenji died, Mrs. Ono changed the the flag in her window from a blue star to a gold one.

"He served his country with bravery and honor," the block manager recited over and over. This speech meant a man had died, and no tribute, flag, or letters of condolence could replace the loss or lessen the anguish. Our words seemed shallow. At lunch, I stood by Mrs. Otaki with her cheeks tear-stained, and her shoulders stooped with sorrow. I tried to speak, but could only muster up a nod.

I wished that the war would end. I wondered if there would be any young men remaining to come home. Would there be anyone left for my sisters to marry? If the war continued much longer, would my teenage brothers, George and Tom, be drafted and sent overseas to wield lethal weapons? And would Mr. Funatake again stand up, unfold the paper, and this time, announce my brothers' names?

❦

The Piano

The official notice gave us one week to sell the business and get rid of all of our possesions except what we could carry. Mrs. Nelson, a friend of many years, crammed two steamer trunks, a bookcase, and three boxes into her small apartment. "I just don't have space for your piano," she lamented, tears streaking down her high cheekbones. "Isn't there anyone who can keep it for you?" Kiyoko shook her head. "Everyone we know has to leave too."

Our Hobart and Cable upright piano was our showpiece. It even had its own room, Room 2, a cozy space with a sofa-bed, a glassed-in bookcase, and a small desk. The piano, clothed in a blue and maroon bench cover and velveteen leg wraps, stood prominently across from the doorway. Every Saturday, my sisters cleaned the keys and buffed the lustrous patina until we could almost see our reflections. Only with permission and soap-scrubbed hands was I allowed to touch the instrument.

Our piano had not been used much in recent years. Neither my brothers nor I had received lessons. The Crash of 1929 had taken its toll on Papa's fortune. It was a reminder of better times when Mama insisted Kiyoko and Shigeko learn to play like proper ladies. She admonished, "You must practice at least ten times every day if you want to perform like your friend, Yoneco." Then she would set out ten matchsticks to help my sisters keep count. After Mama died, when they played familiar tunes from their sheet music, they reminisced about mama's dreams for us. "You must be a good girl," Shigeko would tell me. "Study hard, and always do your best." Mama seemed close by.

With only four days left before we vacated, my sisters pondered where they could find a home for our cherished possession. Meanwhile, the cunning woman who bought our business at far below market value came to our home every day. "Just leave the piano here," she coaxed us. "I'll find a place for it." She had already taken our antique lobby furniture: a library table, a hat rack, an ebony bench, and a gilded mirror. She insisted, "It goes with the business. I'll take care of it." By the following day, she possessed all of our personal appliances, furniture, victrola, and houseware as part of the business inventory. "Don't worry," she kept saying, "I'll take care of it." Papa and Kiyoko, anxious and weary with no time or options left, let it all go, all except for the piano. "*Shoganai* (It can't be helped)," Papa sighed.

As the last day approached, Winifred Fisher, a young woman from the YWCA, unexpectedly appeared. "Is there anything I can do to help?" she offered. When Kiyoko told her about our predicament, she replied, "I already have a spinet in my one bedroom apartment, but I will keep your upright until you return." We had just met Winifred, but her honesty and sincere desire to help won our trust. Our piano was safe. Now, we were ready to leave.

Five years later, after the war ended, we came back to Portland. As promised, Winifred returned our piano. "I'm so sorry," she said. "The finish is badly checked. The only place I could put the piano was by the heater. I did the best I could but I couldn't move it anywhere. I'm sorry." At fifteen, I felt awkward. I couldn't find the right words to express our appreciation. I didn't know how to tell her how my heart skipped a beat when I saw the familiar shape under the protective covering, or how my chest held in my gratitude.

I simply said, "Thank you so much for keeping our piano all these years. I'm sorry it was a bother for you. We are very grateful for your kindness." With embarrassment, I gave her a two-pound box of Russell Stover candy. It was all we could afford.

After Winifred left, I peeled back the front padding. "Ohhh God!" I gasped. Fine mesh cracks veined the dull surface. With my sleeve, I tried to wipe off the whitish haze, but realized it was below the finish. My throat tightened as I continued my inspection. The lower left side bore a chalky white burn, and the exposed legs were chipped and dented. Opening the keyboard, I ran my fingers over the keys. When I hit the familiar flat note, it made me smile. I consoled myself. Like the piano, we were displaced, battered, and forever changed, but at least now we were together again.

Sato Hashizume

Sato Hashizume was born in Japan, raised in Portland, Oregon, and spent her World War II years in Minidoka concentration camp. She is a member of Sigma Theta Tau, the nursing honorary society. She came to San Francisco after graduate studies at the University of Minnesota and was employed by the University of California, San Francisco, where she retired after twenty-six years of service as a teacher, administrator, and nurse practitioner. She served as a nurse educator aboard the ship, USS HOPE, at Sri Lanka. In her retirement years, she is surprised and delighted with the unfolding of her life as she develops the craft of writing.

Fumi Manabe Hayashi

❦

Ashes

In 1931, when I was 5, my older sister, Emi, cut her foot on a tin can. She died four days later; she was just 8 years old.

My parents deeply mourned the loss of their first-born child. Her body was cremated, and her ashes were placed on a piano in our living room. My mother let us trace our fingers over her name, her birth and death dates inscribed in beautiful Old English script. We would open the urn and look inside at the white ashes wrapped in tissue paper. It comforted us to arrange our report cards, birthday greetings, and valentines around her. Emi had picked roses for Mama on Mother's Day just before she died; and ever since then Mama would search the garden for the prettiest rose to place near Emi's urn.

Some time later, California passed a law requiring ashes of the deceased to be kept at a columbarium. After Pearl Harbor, many Japanese graves were vandalized. My parents, already deeply concerned about the conflict between their native land and their adopted land, had the additional worry of protecting Emi's remains. We would not be allowed to take Emi's ashes with us to camp.

Before we were forced to leave Berkeley, we reluctantly placed her urn in a Piedmont columbarium. This would be our second separation from Emi. We had no way of knowing if we would ever be allowed to return to California or when we might reclaim her.

In 1946, our family was finally reunited in our Berkeley home. My mother continued to fret over the placement of Emi's urn at the columbarium. The room was dark and dreary; the urn was placed high to avoid

ABOVE: Fumi Manabe Hayashi, 1944 and 2001.
OPPOSITE: James Takeji Manabe with his children Grace Keiko (in his arms), Emi, and Fumi in front. Berkeley, California, 1930.

possible vandalism. We had not been able to afford a nice place for her, and it would be expensive to move her. I even considered just taking her urn from the niche and bringing her home. But my parents would have been horrified at any defiance of state regulations.

When my dad died in 1983 at the age of 92, we were finally able to afford a grave site close to his for Emi. They rest peacefully in the lovely Heian Garden in El Cerrito, overlooking the beautiful Golden Gate. We visit the site often. And our grandchildren who never knew Emi pick homegrown flowers to decorate her grave as well as that of their beloved grandfather.

❧

Train Ride

I don't know why we had to leave home. Why do we have to carry these things . . . soap, towels, dishes, and even blankets? This sack is so heavy.

Why did I have to leave school? I didn't finish my papers. My homework will be late. I hope Miss Kerry won't be mad. I didn't bring any pencils or my workbook. But maybe I will get a new desk at my new school.

I'm scared of this big train. Smoke is coming out. Mama was crying. Did the train make her feel bad? Will it make us sad? I wonder where the train will take us.

Where is Papa? When will he come back? I hope he comes back soon. How will he find us? Will someone tell him where we went?

Who are these soldiers? They are so tall; they don't move; they don't smile or talk. Those guns are really big.

Nii chan, big brother, told us that we had to get on the train because Japan bombed Pearl Harbor. I think bombing Pearl Harbor was a bad thing. I saw a picture. Maybe Pearl Harbor is airplanes, fire, and boats.

Mama doesn't feel good. She went to the doctor last week. All of those shots are making her sick. *Nii chan* is taking care of her. I hope she gets better soon.

Nii chan packed my pajamas. But he said we couldn't bring Teddy *Kuma*, my Teddy Bear. Santa brought Teddy a long time ago. He sleeps with me every night. Teddy will wait for me. He'll be happy when I come home.

Nii chan knows everything. He will tell us what to do. He will take care of us. *Nii chan* is big. He is 17.

Our Desert Home

With the start of World War II and the Military Evacuation of California, we were hurriedly bussed to the Tanforan Racetrack 50 miles away.

When we first assembled at Tanforan, my father was the only one in our set of horse stalls to have a broom. He had cut down the handle and packed it along with our bedding. All of our many new neighbors borrowed our broom and used it, like us, to clean out the remnants of race horses, the former occupants of our new homes. Our family of six lived in the stall of a single racehorse.

After several months in Tanforan, our daily schedule of waiting became routine and bearable. We waited to use the latrines; we waited in long lines for our meals at the mess halls; we waited to use the laundry room; we waited for the daily head count. We knew that Tanforan was a temporary assembly area so we waited to be sent to a more permanent home in the interior.

We imagined scorpions, dust storms, bad water, and heat. But we thought that surely our permanent camp would be better than our race-

ABOVE: Japanese American family being moved from Tanforan Assembly Center to Topaz, Utah. WRA photograph, National Archives at College Park.

track homes. Maybe we could grow vegetables and fruit for our meals. Our schools might even be equipped with books, tables, desks, and chairs. Our family certainly needed more room.

I had never taken a train ride before. As the day came for our move to an inland camp, I thought that the trip might even be fun. Traveling with family and friends and seeing new places should have been great. However, it soon became boring and tiresome. The curtains were drawn to keep the public from seeing us. We could not watch the passing scene. The train was very old and stuffy. The sandwiches prepared in Tanforan were dry and tasteless. We had to sleep sitting up. My father told us stories to keep us quiet so that others in our car could nap. His stories told of children who did not obey their parents or do their chores. We loved hearing these stories and never once realized he was teaching us how to behave properly.

After riding in a darkened train for two days and one night, we crossed the great Salt Lake. As we passed over the lake, no one could see us, so we were allowed to raise the curtains and look out. As the sun set, reds and golds mixed with the blues of the lake and filled the sky. Our bodies ached from sitting in one spot. Children were upset and crying. An expectant mother cried whenever the train jolted sharply. Parents began losing patience with their children. Cross words were exchanged.

ABOVE: April 29, 1942, Tanforan Assembly Center, San Bruno, California. Line-up of newly arrived internees outside mess hall at noon. Dorothea Lange, WRA photograph, National Archives at College Park.

Finally we were allowed to leave the train. The soldiers formed a long line, facing us, their rifles ready. They watched our every move.

I had never been in a desert like Topaz with rows of tar-papered barracks and dust blowing everywhere. In Tanforan, we were surrounded by rows of trees and grassy mountains. We had built a garden with a lake in the infield of the racetrack. In Tanforan, a former neighbor brought us brooms, buckets, soap, and mops. Friends could visit us at Tanforan, but Topaz was like a place that God had forgotten.

As soon as we got to our assigned room, my father began to mop and clean. As soon as he finished mopping, a layer of dust coated everything. He went back and forth, filling his bucket at the central latrine. He mopped and swept again and again. My mother joined him by arranging and rearranging six cots, packing crates, clothes, and personal belongings into our new 20 x 20 ft. space.

I realized that we could keep our room clean, but would we ever be able to make this place feel like our home?

❦

There's No Place Like Home

The vast skies over the Central Utah desert were a deep azure blue. Sunsets drenched Topaz and the surrounding miles of desert with brilliant shades of reds, yellows, and orange. Distant mountains representing lost freedom seemed to beckon us. And the night skies were filled with stars—far brighter, larger, and more numerous than those that filled the skies over our former California homes.

Located in Whirlwind Valley, enclosed by barbed wire and armed guards, Topaz was often engulfed by swirling winds and dust storms that blotted out the sun and permeated our eyes, noses, and every inch of our homes.

One night, I was returning to my barrack room. The roads were coated with frozen mud and snow. Icicles hung from the barrack roofs, and smoke rose from many chimneys. It would soon be our second Christmas in detention.

I felt homesick for my California Christmas. I wanted a pine tree on a wooden stand. I wanted its branches filled with cotton for snow and aluminum icicles. I wanted glass-blown fruit of many colors to brighten the tree. I wanted artificial holly, garlands of red and green cellophane, and many colored lights to sparkle.

I missed Shattuck Avenue in downtown Berkeley. I wanted to look

TOPAZ, UTAH

into store windows decorated for Christmas. How would it feel to actually use one of those beautifully wrapped bath powders or colognes? What would it be like to soak in a hot bath in a room with a door and no line of people impatiently waiting for me to vacate the tub? I longed to hear Christmas carols everywhere. I wanted to be enticed by material things.

Topaz—no display windows, no red or green lights, no Christmas trees. Topaz—uniformly charcoal grey and dull, without music. How long would we stay here? Would we be detained for yet a third Christmas? When would we be able to go home and celebrate the Holiday season with our families and friends? And when would we again enjoy our family favorite, turkey with lots of hot rice and gravy?

Note: "There's no place like home" is a line taken from the song "Home Sweet Home," written by Sir Henry Rowley Bishop in London in 1821.

ABOVE: 1943, Aerial view of Topaz concentration camp. The camp, which held approximately 8,100 Japanese Americans, was built in the barren desert of central Utah. This photo was taken by a Topaz internee and was sold in the camp co-op. It is from a three-postcard set that, when combined, creates an aerial panoramic view.

Fumi Manabe Hayashi

In 1926, Fumi Manabe was born to Salvation Army Captains Takeji and Chitose Manabe in Oakland, California. The family moved to Berkeley and soon after, they became members of the Christian Layman Church. The second of five children, she entered kindergarten speaking little English.

She was interned at the Tanforan Racetrack Assembly Center and The Central Utah Relocation Center, Topaz, from April 1942 to December 1944.

Fumi met Tad Hayashi at Tanforan. They were a married after he finished his army tour of duty in Japan as a member of the intelligence unit under General MacArthur. They raised three children in Berkeley. Both were active in many community groups.

Fumi Hayashi is currently spending her retirement years enjoying classes at the Japanese American Services of the East Bay Senior Center and visiting with family and friends. The effort of recalling and recording her World War II experiences has been challenging and rewarding.

Florence Miho Nakamura

The Living Room

It was my favorite room in our apartment before the war. During summer vacations, I would run to the grocery store across the street, buy a small French roll, and cut it in half. Then I'd slather oodles of butter on each side, place it in the broiler of the stove until it was toasted to the perfect shade of brown. I brought this delicacy to the living room where I sat on the floor between the easy chair and the large console radio to listen to the soap opera "Stella Dallas" until noon. I sat on a plush oriental rug with lots of rich red shades and an intricate design I traced with my fingers, while listening to the exciting lives on the radio and breakfasting on the delicious roll. I avidly followed the adventures of the characters, fantasizing how they looked and dressed. In those days of the late 1930s and early 1940s, television was unheard of, and we used our imagination to bring the characters such as Captain Midnight to life. We waited for the end of the show when he would give us a mystery message to solve on our Captain Midnight Decoder. It was usually simple and had a positive theme. After spending the morning by the radio, it was time to have lunch and go off to meet my friends for the rest of the afternoon.

Occasionally my sister would join me with a book that she was reading, but we enjoyed looking out of the large front window, watching people go by. Very often, a young man watched us from across the street. As he sat on the steps, he looked longingly at our window, hoping to get a glimpse of my pretty sister.

In 1942, we were sent to the Tanforan Racetrack in San Bruno, California, and then to Topaz concentration camp in Utah. Our living

ABOVE: Florence Miho Nakamura, 1944 and 2001.
OPPOSITE TOP: Florence (circled), Eighth grade core class, Topaz Jr. High, Spring 1943. OPPOSITE BOTTOM: Florence with Harry Nakamura, Topaz War Relocation Center, Summer 1945. Photo by T. Sakurai.

room and bedroom was one bare room for our family of five. We shared a communal latrine, shower, and laundry with over one hundred other inmates, and we ate at the mess hall with those people. We had no living room where we were able to talk, study, and enjoy ourselves. What a horrible place to be. A prison for families.

❧

Arrival in Tanforan

Our family number was 19153. In April 1942, on the day of departure, each member of my family had a cardboard tag with this number attached to his or her coat. This tag was our identification for the dura-tion of our incarceration.

From our apartment at Pine and Webster Streets, our family walked down the hill to *Kinmon Gakuen*, the site of one of San Francisco's Japanese language schools. We joined the large group assembled in front of the building for our journey to an unknown destination. Everybody was dressed as if they were headed to church. The women wore dark dresses with white collars beneath their coats and their Sunday shoes. The men wore suits with white shirts, ties, hats, and dress shoes. The boys were decked out in slacks, shirts, jackets, and caps. The girls wore dresses, skirts and blouses, and saddle shoes. Along with my two sisters, Mary and Kiki, I had heard rumors that the grounds were muddy, so we wore our brand new tan majorette boots with tassels in front. These were purchased just prior to our departure for protection from the unknown perils which lay before us. The sidewalk was covered with

belongings wrapped in bedspreads, stuffed into cardboard boxes and dilapidated suitcases.

A string of buses were lined up, one behind the other. Soldiers carried rifles to guard and keep us under control although their presence was just a formality. We were a quiet and orderly group, standing in lines waiting to board. We were not going to start a riot or try to run away.

As we boarded the bus, curious spectators lined up across the street. No one waved to us as we rode away.

Although I don't recall the bus ride, I do remember our arrival in Tanforan. The driver brought us through a gate which closed behind us with a clang. As we got off the bus, we found ourselves in a large area amidst a sea of friendly Japanese faces. I didn't know where we were, but I was not frightened because I was with my family—my father, my mother and my two older sisters. With them, I felt safe.

My eyes were drawn to the north, and I saw a large sign on the side of the mountain which read,

SOUTH
SAN FRANCISCO
THE INDUSTRIAL CITY

After we were sent to Topaz concentration camp in Utah, the racetrack of Tanforan was occupied by the military. When World War II ended, it was again a racetrack and later became a shopping mall. The sign is still on that mountain, but every time I return from my son's house on the peninsula, I turn away from this reminder of a painful experience.

ABOVE: Street view of "South San Francisco, The Industrial City" sign on San Bruno hill.
OPPOSITE: 1942. San Francisco Bay Area Japanese Americans, most of whom were U.S. citizens, board busses for Tanforan Assembly Center. Luggage was limited to what internees could carry. Most other possessions (homes, cars, property, businesses) were lost or sold at "fire sales" for a fraction of their worth. Photo courtesy of Grace Oshita.

❦

Barrack in Tanforan

After our family was processed into Tanforan, we were "escorted" by Andy, one of the Nisei youths who volunteered to direct incoming families. He led us to our barrack next to the high cyclone fence topped with barbed wire. We could see El Camino Real on the other side. It had rained the previous day, and the racetrack was a quagmire. Boards were placed over the mud, and we walked carefully on top of them, trying not to fall off.

Inside our barrack, there were five metal cots with mattresses and folded army blankets. My parents, two sisters, and I stood in the center of the room wondering what to do next. Our linens were wrapped and bundled in a large bedspread. We made our beds and tried to put our possessions in order. There were neither dressers nor closets to put our clothing in, so we substituted our suitcases for furniture. Later, the men built chests and other furnishings. My father was not a very good carpenter and one night the shelves that he constructed fell down, along with our dishes, making a loud crash which could be heard throughout the barrack.

We were housed in one of the newly constructed barracks. It was the first time in my life that I lived in a place that no one else had ever occupied. The rooms were separated by plywood walls, their upper edges bordering the sloped roof. There was no place for privacy. After a few days, the internees broke down cardboard boxes that they had appropriated and nailed them over each open space. We were one of the "lucky" families—we could have been housed in the horse stalls which reeked with odors left by the previous occupants.

Since the barracks were identical, the door would often open, and strangers would come into our room, then sheepishly back out. "Oops. Sorry, wrong unit."

My sister and I were not accustomed to communal bathing and had only taken baths at home, so the open showers were very daunting. We didn't even know how to take a shower. To solve this problem, we got a hold of a huge galvanized tub and carried it to the shower room. We filled the tub with water from the shower and took turns, scrunched up and washing ourselves in our "bathtub." It was far from comfortable, but we were clean. The neighbors laughed as the two of us came running down the road every evening, in time for roll call, the tub swinging between us.

☙

Eucalyptus Trees

Last Sunday, after the rain, I stood by five dripping eucalyptus trees and waited to be rescued by my husband. I had locked my handbag inside the car, the keys peeking out from an open zipper. How thankful I felt to be in the presence of the trees, their forms absent all the years I was incarcerated in the desert of Utah among sagebrush and shrubs.

Looking down at the sidewalk, I noticed a manhole-sized plaque honoring Mary Ellen "Mammy" Pleasant who was known as the Mother of Civil Rights. The plaque had been placed at the western terminus of the Underground Railroad for fugitive slaves escaping from the south. She had planted the five eucalyptus trees where I now stood, no longer in camp, yet thinking of freedom and its meaning to anyone who has lost it. The trunk of one of the trees swirled in an unusual sweeping design, resembling the rope lava of the Kilauea Cauldron on the island of Hawaii.

Moving to the next two trees, I noticed that the long, exposed roots of one tree had grown and touched the roots of the other. They appeared to be holding hands. I was happy to imagine that they were not lonely. Engrossed in my musing, I didn't notice my husband's arrival until he blew the horn of the car to get my attention.

For over sixty years, I've walked by those trees, on the way to church and Japanese school and on the way home, kicking the acorn-like seeds scattered on the sidewalk, only now seeing the trees and the beauty of nature's work.

☙

Florence Miho Nakamura

Florence Miho Nakamura was born in South Park, San Francisco, on July 12, 1929. She is the youngest of three daughters of Shime and Shizuko Miho.

Florence lived in San Francisco until her internment at Tanforan Assembly Center in San Bruno, California, and later in Topaz War Relocation Center in Utah. She was eleven years of age when she was sent to camp and sixteen years old by the time she returned to San Francisco. Florence and Harry, her husband of fifty-two years, reside in San Francisco where they are enjoying a wonderful retirement. They have two grown children: Sharen, their daughter, and Scott, their son. Florence's five grandchildren are the "joys of her life."

In the Internment Autobiography Writing Workshop, she has had the opportunity to express her World War II experiences for her family and future generations. She thanks Brian for his direction and encouragement.

Ruth Y.Okimoto

The Rattlesnake and Scorpion
A Desert Home, Poston, Arizona 1942

Said the Scorpion to the Rattlesnake,
"What manner of commotion is happening here?
The sawing of lumber and pounding of nails,
    black tar-paper falls and covers my trail.
Tall fence posts pierce deep into the ground
    securing chainlink fences and barbed wire from town."

Said the Rattlesnake to the Scorpion,
"Indeed, huge pipes obstruct and crisscross my path,
    and loud swishing noises disturb my sleep.
Why, I went forging for food and found
    my favorite hunting ground vanished today
    and more will dwindle, I've heard them say."

Said the Scorpion to the Rattlesnake,
"And worse even yet, small human fingers foolishly grab
    my sisters, brothers, cousins, and all,
    and drown them in jars filled with alcohol."
"Why foolish, indeed," replied the Rattlesnake,
    "don't they know of your sting, my venomous bite?"

ABOVE: Ruth Y. Okimoto, 1944 and 2001.
OPPOSITE TOP & BOTTOM: Poston, Arizona, 1942. Fred Clark, WRA photograph, National Archives at College Park.

Ruth with her
brothers: Joe (left),
Paul (back),
Dan (front).
Poston Camp III,
Fall 1943.

Said the Scorpion to the Rattlesnake,
"What kind of human would dare intrude into our sacred place?
We've lived on this land for centuries, I'm told,
    so why do they come here to ravage and destroy?
We've lived in peace, both you and I,
    with no intent to hurt or annoy."

Said the Rattlesnake to the Scorpion,
"Some humans, I'm told, regard those who differ in skin
    or thought with what they call 'justifiable' hate."
"As you know," continued the Rattlesnake,
    "humans are the most dangerous animal of all;
    they kill with lethal weapons ten feet tall."

Asked the Scorpion of the Rattlesnake,
"So what do you think they are building here,
    in the midst of our desert home?"
Answered the Rattlesnake with a somber voice,
"It's something menacing, and I fear
    portends of dangers yet unclear."

Magazine Pictures
A Nikkei Perspective

'Twas 1954, the year of my graduation
    a most exciting year filled with anticipation.
"The world's your oyster," the commencement
    speaker said, "with untold fortunes and pearls to cultivate."

But sex and gender roles we learned as babes
    in our parents' arms set the stage.
Boys play with fast-moving cars and trucks.
Girls play with dolls, serve tea in tiny cups.

A man faces challenges and competition;
    reacts with speed to a fast-moving world.
He must be quick and agile, ready to pounce
    lest he gets tagged unfit and squeezed out.

A woman sits sedately priming her hair;
    protects her skin to ensure a pretty face.
She takes care lest she loses her sex appeal,
    a precious and priceless commodity for sale.

'Twas 1954, the year of my graduation
    a most exciting year filled with anticipation.
"The world's your oyster," the commencement
    speaker said, "with untold fortunes and pearls to cultivate."

Nikkei youth went dancing to the sounds
    of big brass bands despite their parents' objection.
Memories of guard towers and barbed wire fence
    unleashed a strong need for transformation.

We are all Americans. Can't you see?
We play the same sports, understand competition.
We even have beauty pageants, lay bare our skin,
    and share America's obsession with being thin.

But real estate agents professed out loud,
    "Japs would contaminate our white neighborhood."
"Don't move here," their directive said.
    So we searched again and moved elsewhere instead.

'Twas 1998, the year of my graduation,
    a most exciting year filled with anticipation.
"The world's a global village," the commencement
    speaker said, "it's time to change, expand prior thinking."

But sex and gender roles we learned as babes
    in our parents' arms set the stage.
Men play with fast-moving cars and utility trucks.
Women obsess with fashion, serve tea in ceramic cups.

Messages from most politicians still often say,
    "Don't come here; move on without delay."
Racial and gender prejudice still prevail
    Worthy legislation and intentions get derailed.

Magazine pictures scream out loud.
We face competition; must react to a nanosecond world.
We color our hair, use chemical peels, drugs and knives
    to keep the promises of youth and sex alive.

Ruth Y. Okimoto, Ph.D.

Ruth Yoshiko Okimoto was six years old when U.S. soldiers escorted her family to the Santa Anita Assembly Center on May 1, 1942. During the family's stay in Santa Anita, her mother gave birth to a baby boy in a makeshift delivery room in the Santa Anita Racetrack. Two weeks later, the family was shipped by train to the "Poston Relocation Project" on the Colorado River Indian Reservation. There, her family lived for the next three years in Poston Camp III. After the war, her family returned to San Diego on September 11, 1945.

Prior to returning to graduate school in 1991, Ruth worked as a college adminis-trator, a human resource manager in a large corporation, and as an independent career counselor. She holds a B.A. from Mills College and an M.A. and Ph.D. from the California School of Professional Psychology.

Today, Ruth and her husband, Marvin Lipofsky, live in Berkeley, California. She is the mother of three grown children and one stepdaughter; grandmother to a grandson and two step-grandchildren.

"Magazine Pictures" was inspired by the Japanese American National Museum's 1997 Calendar – June. In the years after World War II, a number of magazines put out by and aimed at young Nisei adults appeared. Scene, the longest running of these, was published in Chicago by some of the leading lights of Nisei journalism and featured articles and pictures highlighting Nisei success and achievement.

Yoshito Wayne Osaki

The Tackling Dummy

The football coach was my Math teacher when I was a freshman at Clarksburg High School. One day he said to me, "Are you going to come out for football next season?" I was just a skinny kid and somewhat "chicken." The next season I went out for football, not knowing what to expect. Coach was a huge man; he was an ex-college football lineman and an ex-Olympic shotputter. On the football field he became a different person, no longer the gentle teacher he was in the classroom. He yelled at players like a drill sergeant in the U.S. Marine Corps with fire spitting out of his mouth. The practices were grueling and made my whole body ache. Coach constantly yelled at me when I forgot plays or didn't block hard enough. "Osaki, put on the pads," he'd say. "Oh my gosh, not again," I said to myself. Then one by one, the entire team practiced tackling on me.

I wondered why Coach picked me to be the tackling dummy. It was not only physically painful, but I felt somewhat humiliated and resentful. No white players were ever ordered by Coach to be the tackling dummy. Maybe Coach thought I needed toughening up.

After practice, I'd pull off my sweaty jersey and pants and take a shower. Sometimes when I could not get a ride, I had to walk home, which was about eight miles away. I did not get home until dark and was too tired for homework.

At the games, Coach did not play me at all, not even for one second. That first year of football was really rough on me, but at least I stuck it out. Because I did not have any fun that year, I decided not to go out for football the following year. Instead I signed up for P.E. class where the

ABOVE: Yoshito Wayne Osaki, 1939 and 2001.
OPPOSITE: Wayne standing in front of the Osaki family's barrack, 1946.

instructor asked, "How come you didn't go out for football? Our football team has a good chance of making it to the championship." At the urging of the P.E. instructor, I went back to football. I also had a hunch that Coach wanted me back because, the second time I tried out, I didn't have to be the tackling dummy. However, he chose another Nisei rookie to become the tackling dummy. Was it easier for Coach to ask any non-protesting player to be the tackling dummy or was he singling out us Nisei? And why did he not choose the better Nisei players for this thankless, painful job? Was I not expendable because Coach was using the platoon system for the first time and needed more players on both offense and defense?

That year I started at defensive back. Our defensive team did not allow any team to score in all the league games. I even played on the offensive team at times. On one occasion, I scored a conversion after a touchdown. Coach called the play: "25S." I received the ball in the fullback position and faked a handoff. As I hit the hole, an opposing linebacker grabbed my shoulder, but I tore away from him and plunged across the goal line for the point after. Finally, Coach gave me a chance to have one moment of glory.

In the postseason game, we played against the rival Cortland team who, in the past, had beaten us every year. This time, we beat them 25 to 0. Our football team won the championship for the first time in school history. The year was 1941. Just days after the football season, Pearl Harbor was bombed.

❧

My Dog "Teny"

One day my father brought home a puppy, and I named him "Teny." He was like a fuzzy ball, with light tan fur on his back and short white fur underneath. He was my constant companion. When I came home from school, he was always there waiting for me, wagging his tail, and jumping all over me. When I played harmonica, he sat by me and accompanied me with his off-key howl. He was always with me when I went fishing, hunting, or just for a walk. He was just a mutt, but to me he was the cutest dog in the whole wide world. He was my best friend.

When the Evacuation Order came in late May of 1942, we were told no pets were allowed in camp. Who would take care of my Teny after we were gone? Who would feed him? Who would be willing to take care of a "Jap" dog? We had no choice but to leave him behind.

A few days before we were to leave for camp, he looked so sad all day long. He would not even eat his favorite food: rice and meat with gravy. Somehow he knew that he would be left behind. The day before our departure, he disappeared. I searched everywhere, calling his name, but I could not find him.

Finally the day came, and we loaded our duffel bags and suitcases into the back of the truck. I climbed on top of the baggage to look for Teny, still hoping to see him for the last time. As the truck started to speed up, Teny suddenly leaped out of nowhere and chased us. After about a mile, he became tired and started to fall behind. Finally he stopped and sat down in the middle of the road, panting heavily. Tears filled my eyes, and I could no longer see my Teny.

❦

The Paper Christmas Tree

White snow covered the grounds, the roofs, and the hills. Long icicles hung from the eaves, and smoke rose from hundreds of chimneys. This scene could have been from a Christmas card, but no, this was Tule Lake concentration camp, U.S.A. We were in the middle of an icy desert. There was not a tree in sight, just sagebrush as far as I could see. This was a Christmas season with no cheer, just dark clouds hanging over our camp.

How could I create a Christmas mood? I headed to Canteen #1 at Ward 4, where my older brother was a manager. With my monthly clothing allowance check of $3.50, I bought a set of construction paper in various colors. Back in our barracks, I cut up the dark green paper and glued the pieces into a shape of a Christmas tree. Small round shapes—in red, orange, yellow, pink, and chartreuse—were snipped from the paper and pasted on the tree to look like ornaments.

This paper Christmas tree was only about a foot tall, but it did help to brighten up the mood of our first Christmas behind barbed wire fences and guard towers. Finally, I was able to say, "Merry Christmas."

❦

The Loyalty Oath

During the pre-World War II days, I felt proud to be a Nisei. Our parents taught us to take pride in our Japanese heritage, but also to respect and emulate people such as George Washington and Abraham Lincoln. I took pride in being the product of two cultures.

After the bombing of Pearl Harbor, I was numb for a while. However, I realized that I must prove my loyalty to the United States of America, the country of my birth and citizenship. I registered for the Draft immediately and received a classification of 1A. After I was incarcerated in Tule Lake concentration camp, I again registered for the Draft, but this time I was reclassified as 4C, "Enemy Alien." This puzzled me greatly. I thought my U.S. citizenship had been taken away by the U.S. government.

When the Loyalty Oath was announced, I thought I had already registered for the Draft twice. There should have been no question as to my intent to serve in the U.S. Military Forces. We had heard of the 100th Battalion from Hawaii being wiped out. Why would the U.S. government try to recruit an "Enemy Alien"? Some thought that this might be a plot for genocide. Did "foreswearing" allegiance to the Emperor mean confession of previous loyalty to the Emperor? Was I now changing my loyalty to the U.S.? Did the answer of "Yes" in any way imply consent to the incarceration and evacuation? These were only a few of our many questions.

A committee was formed, and they asked these questions to the Camp Director. He refused to answer. "I don't give a damn how you answer the Loyalty Oath," he stated. "But if you don't answer it, you will be put into the Isolation Camp for twenty years."

His arrogance and the threat of Isolation Camp created a tense situation. Subsequently a group of young men who refused the Loyalty Oath were picked up and thrown into a jail at a nearby town.

Anger and fear reached a hysterical level. I can still hear the mess hall bells ringing all over camp, day and night, calling for block meetings to deal with the crisis. The Camp Director set a deadline date, and now we were under tremendous pressure. I waited until the last day and answered "No, No" in protest to the Camp Director. I did not know how my father, mother, brother, and sister answered. We never talked about it.

Protests by many internees and the poor handling of the Loyalty Oath by the Camp Director led to his firing. After school reopened, our high school English teacher assigned us an essay on "Camp Problems." Some wrote of family problems. Others wrote of crime or juvenile delinquency. I wrote about the Loyalty Oath. Much to my surprise, my essay was selected as one of the two to be made into a class drama. I still remember the last sentence of my essay: "Some day I hope that true Americans will understand why I answered 'No, No.'"

Note: In 1988, the U.S. government apologized and issued monetary redress to all Japanese Americans who were forcibly removed from the West Coast and interned during World War II, including the Issei and those who responded "No, No" or refused to answer the questionnaire. After I was released from Tule Lake camp, I enlisted in the U.S. Marine Corps Active Reserve.

Leaving

The day before I left Tule Lake, a family friend asked me to delay my schedule one day, so I could help them with their baggage and their children. They had been family friends for many years, and the wife was the daughter of my father's best friend. My father and he had gone to the same high school at Hamada City in Shimane-ken and had farmed together near Courtland from early 1900 to 1929.

The couple had three small children and a baby. I felt sorry for their predicament, but I was anxious to leave the camp. I had already scheduled a visit to my parents in San Francisco on the way to New York. I could have checked to see if I could change my departure to a day later, since I knew the person at the Relocation Office who handled the train scheduling. But even a one day delay felt unbearable to me. I promised them that I would meet them at the Richmond, California train station the next day to help them settle. I left them still begging me as I closed the door on them.

Later that day, I picked up a stick and dug a hole in the ground outside our barrack. Then I placed my diary in the hole and buried it. I wanted to leave behind every bitter memory of Tule Lake. For almost four years, I had written entries in my diary: about the pain of segregation and the separation from close friends; about being pressured by the radical elements to renounce my citizenship; about the oppressive loyalty oath, the choking tear gas, the freezing stockade, the confusing renunciation, and the threat of deportation by the Justice Department. But I also had written about good moments, sports, fond memories, and the first love of my youth behind the barbed wire fence.

Next, I went around to say goodbye to my few friends and others

who were still in the desolate camp, waiting to be shipped to unknown destinations. The following day, I boarded the bus. After a short distance, it stopped at the last gate. Probably the stop was for just a few minutes, but to me it was like an eternity. I held my breath. Why did the bus stop? I wondered. Perhaps the bus would turn back and unload us. Finally the bus started to move, and I took a deep breath. I left Tule Lake concentration camp on March 12, 1946.

I thought of nothing but leaving. I was so anxious to get out. Yet I couldn't forget my family friends' predicament or let go of my guilt. My shame only worsened after I boarded the train which took me back on the same track that had taken me to Tule Lake many years ago. The train ride was rather uneventful, but I continued to feel guilty about the family friend who had asked me to help them.

Also I recalled that Sidoris McCartney, whom I'd worked with at the Relocation Office in Tule Lake, was waiting for me to say farewell at the Klamath Falls train station. He treated me to a lunch at the nearby restaurant. It was strange and uncomfortable for me to be eating with white people all around me. I can still remember how good the roast beef sandwich tasted. After almost four years, this was my first meal outside of camp, my first taste of freedom.

ABOVE: July 1, 1942. A panoramic view of Tule Lake concentration camp, Newell, California, south of the Oregon border. Francis Stewart, WRA photograph, National Archives at College Park.

❧

Yoshito Wayne Osaki

Yoshito Wayne Osaki was born near Courtland, California, in 1923 and attended seg-regated Oriental Grammar School. After seventh grade, he transferred to integrated Clarksburg Grammar School. When Pearl Harbor was bombed, he was a junior at Clarksburg High School. His family was sent to Tule Lake concentration camp, where they stayed for the duration of World War II. Wayne's camp experiences inspired his concern for civil rights, and he helped to rebuild the Japanese American community after the war.

He studied Architecture at UC Berkeley, where he graduated with honors in 1951. That same year, he became a Christian. He established a private practice in 1958 in San Francisco and designed more than sixty-five churches throughout Northern California. Many of the ethnic churches he designed reflect the cultural heritages of their congrega-tions. He was also involved in the design of schools. He believes religion and education can help improve society and, as a result, lead to a more harmonious world.

After forty years of private practice designing various types of buildings, he is now semi-retired, but is still active with the concerns of the community. He is married to Sally Noda, who is originally from Selma, California. He is the father of four sons: Glenn, Paul, Dean, and Jon, and a grandfather of three grandchildren: Shannon, Mika and Lee. He is currently writing his own autobiography and family history, and he has found the Internment Autobiography Writing Workshop helpful in this process.

Toru Saito

❦

Owada's Market
(an excerpt)

A sharp tapping sound pierced through the open double doors of Owada's Market, a Japanese fish and grocery store across from the old Post Street Buddhist Church, the heart of Japantown, San Francisco. It was late spring. The patchy morning fog lingered until eleven before yielding to a pale blue sky. As if driven by machine, Mr. Owada's weathered hands were flipping heads of nappa cabbage, all face up and in neat straight rows. "Keep the produce fresh and clean and customers will buy," he liked to say. His market was the most popular in J-Town, and he was determined to keep it that way. It was silent in the old market except for the static-ridden wails of Big Band music drifting out of the back room from the little Philco radio, barely audible over the groans of the walk-in refrigerator and the rhythmic *whick . . . whick . . .* of the overhead paddle fan just inside the front doors.

The tapping sound distracted Owada, and he turned in time to observe a big white man in an army uniform hammering the last tack to a notice on the telephone pole in front of his market. The moment he saw the man, a tingle of fear ran through him. A white man in J-Town was usually cause for concern, especially one in uniform. His curiosity soon turned to resentment as he remembered the punches he received as a youngster from the white bullies on the schoolyard and the racist names they called him as he walked home from school.

His eyes lowered to the base of the pole where he had stacked boxes of fresh strawberries. "Better not be stepping on my strawberries," he said to himself, his anger beginning to grow. "What is this," he thought,

ABOVE: Toru Saito, c. 1940 and 2001.
OPPOSITE: Toru with his mother, Kikue Saito, 1939. Photograph by Kazumo Motomi.

"a white man in an army uniform in J-Town." He looked the man over, frozen in place at the produce bin. "*Ketoh no chikuso* (S.O.B)," he muttered.

Owada ran the market as if his property line extended well into the street, which it did not. The sight of the white man hammering on his telephone pole made him physically rigid with rage. "*Ketoh no chikuso*," he whispered again, still incensed over the incidents a month ago in April when he was accused of "cheating the Government" by the California Sales Tax Collector and fined one hundred ninety dollars for "sales tax owed." Owada kept his books in strict order and conscientiously paid every penny he ever owed the City, County, and the State. This large fine was unprecedented and caused him a great deal of shame and grief, yet he did not protest due to his respect for the authority of the Government. Only the Japanese-owned markets were targeted in this manner. A week later, his Beer and Wine license was revoked by the State. The official explanation was: "Found to be of Japanese ancestry." Now it was just a matter of time. He was essentially out of business at this point. He could no longer compete with his white competitors, yet he refused to surrender.

"*Ketoh no chikuso*," he muttered louder. He felt his resentment swell in his stomach. However, a history of negative results from conflicts with whites reinforced the motto of his peers, "Why fight? You can't win. Waste time." He knew anywhere outside of J-Town was the "*hakujin's* (white person's) world," but here in J-Town it was a different story. "This is my place," he would shout in the privacy of his back room. "I was born here, grew up here, married here, raised my kids here, and I will die here. I pay my share of taxes and obey all laws, and still I live in segregation and am treated like a second class citizen. I'm not allowed to swim in Fleishacker Pool, not allowed to bathe at Sutro's bath house, or even reserve a room at the big hotels downtown. So what wrong did I do?" He knew the answer. He knew the answer all too well. He just had to blow off steam every now and then to maintain his sanity.

It took him a few minutes to cool down after the man moved out of sight toward Fillmore Street. Owada stepped cautiously to the storefront and peered down Post Street between the crates of green onions and gobo stacked high on the sidewalk against the front windows. His eyes scanned the sidewalk for the large army uniform that would have towered above the shorter local residents. Satisfied the man was gone, he stepped out to examine the placard. Tilting his head back, he read the bold words of the heading: "INSTRUCTIONS TO ALL PERSONS OF JAPANESE ANCESTRY."

Shocked by the heading, he grabbed an empty orange crate and stepped onto the thin slats for a closer look, his legs trembling. He squinted at the smaller print as perspiration beaded across his face. His glasses began to fog and slide down his wet nose. He struggled to keep his balance. He could not believe what he was clearly reading: "May 5, 1942. All persons of Japanese ancestry, both alien and non-alien, will be evacuated from the above area by 12:00 noon P.W.T. Monday, May 11, 1942."

"Why that's only six days from now!!" he exclaimed. "And what's a 'non-alien'? Why, that has to be a . . . CITIZEN! That's it, a CITIZEN?? That means me!" he gasped. "This can't be right, I must have read it wrong."

He read it again, and each time it read the same. It was signed, "The Lieutenant General of the U.S. Army, J. L. DeWitt." He was in shock. "What about my store? My new truck? My family? My house?" he wondered out loud. "That army uniform was genuine, just like the one I wore when I volunteered for the service," he thought. "Is this legal? No! It can't be!!" he argued at the printed words. Overwhelmed, Owada swayed precariously atop the flimsy crate, its slats ready to snap. Likewise, Owada's mental stability dangled in jeopardy. Yet unknown to him were the greater misfortunes that were still to come.

❦

End of the Line

The rickety, ancient train, covered with dust, slowed to a sudden mid-desert stop. Filled to capacity, it lurched backwards violently, forcing the Japanese prisoners' heads to bow in unison to the military police in charge. A volt of fear flashed through the train. Dozing heads were snapped wide awake. Everyone sat up at attention as if ordered by an angry drill sergeant. Something was about to happen; we all sensed it. No one spoke for fear of triggering the rage of the hostile white soldiers who glared at us with threatening eyes. Then, as if on cue, the silence was broken by the wail of a newborn baby, jolted awake inside her mother's arms. "Where the heck are we?" a teenage boy's voice whispered from behind cautiously. "End of the line," his Kibei father muttered with a thick accent. The sighs were clear, "This is it" . . . we had arrived.

Even with the windows open, the ventilation system was inadequate and suffocating . . . and coughing could be heard throughout the train. Then a slight breeze moved slowly through the packed train like an answered prayer. The stagnant air was thick with the smell of our mothball-laden clothing. We were sticky wet with perspiration. The additional body heat of the nervous prisoners aboard only magnified the misery. Because all information of our travel and destination was kept secret from us, we had prepared for the most severe, cold conditions. Everyone was dressed in heavy overcoats, winter hats, and extra sweaters. We underestimated the wrath and willful oversight of our government. No one suspected a journey of three days and two nights across California, Nevada, and halfway through Utah. That distance from the only home we knew, Japantown, San Francisco, could have only been imagined on a "dream vacation." We looked ridiculous, dressed like Christmas shoppers in the blazing Sevier Desert, Millard County, Utah. We had to have looked comical, but no one dared to laugh.

Suddenly, the order came, "Everyone up!" We struggled to our forgotten feet and strained to reach our bulky bundles with numb arms. We squeezed down the narrow aisle towards the exit at the rear of the coach; then down the steel stairs we stumbled to freedom, space, elbow room, the vast salt flats, the scorching desert floor. Blinded by the glaring sun, we staggered to keep our balance, and we felt a sting in our noses from the dry heat.

"This way! This way!" the soldiers screamed, forming a picket fence of bayonets, which were fixed at the ends of rifles. The usually controlled J-town residents reacted like ants vacating a disturbed nest. Instinctually, we scrambled to locate family members. Then we followed closely behind mama and papa's lead, and my older sister Akiko dutifully kept us four younger ones together while burdened by two heavy suitcases. To our credit, we were able to think clearly despite the nightmare of having loaded guns aimed at us for the first time. We plotted by non-verbal communication for what seemed our only hope for survival. We were funneled into a single column and formed a monstrous human serpent that snaked through the maze of sagebrush then extended as far as we could see through the distorting heat waves. The heat from the ground burned through the soles of our shoes. With each step our feet sunk deeper into the sandy silt, and soon our shoes disappeared completely. Now, all was silent except for the rhythmic zippering sounds of the sagebrush against our corduroy pants.

We shuffled past the soldiers with our heads bowed, avoiding eye contact. We peered over the tops of our glasses, scanning only left and right. Our feet shuffled like penguins' feet, avoiding the heels of those in front. We moved to the muted rhythm of a deadly march. Like cattle being herded to slaughter, our feelings were numb with powerlessness as we were pushed and prodded ahead. Gradually the barbed wire fencing came into view, and the tall guard towers looming above made us realize that, although we were innocent of any crime, we were being led into a . . . prison . . . a concentration camp. I turned to Mama, her beautiful face never lied. She could always say so much with just a glance. "Don't ask me . . . I don't know," her answer came . . . Was it possible . . . could this really be happening to us . . . or could this be . . . just a bad dream?

❧

Hidden Testimony

In the chill of the 3:00 a.m. darkness, October 28, 1945, we huddled out front as Mama locked the door for the last time—our life in America's concentration camp was over. We took our final look at the black tar-paper barrack that had barely spared us from the minus 30 degree winters and had baked us alive in the 110 degree summers. It appeared empty and sad in the dim light. Then she and papa, with the five of us children, stepped back, lined up, and bowed farewell together to Building 10, Block 4, Topaz, Utah. We paused, turned, and slowly walked away—we didn't look back. We were forced out by "Military Orders," as we were forced in three years earlier by "Military Orders," taking only what we could carry by hand.

"Topaz? You mean that ol' relocation center?" the paunchy blond Utah Highway Patrolman whined. "Why that's in the Sevier Desert, one hundred and forty miles south of Salt Lake City and seventeen miles west of Delta. But there ain't nutten there," he said as he directed me to my destination. But he never told me about that last stretch of abandoned Millard County road that bucked and rattled my new 1995 Toyota to a dusty stop. I waited for the dust to clear then got out. I had finally made it! I had reached the end of my fifty-year trek back to Topaz.

The summer sun felt like it had dipped lower than usual and was blazing just above my head. The place was sizzling. Although it was bone-dry, the heat waves gave the illusion of an eerie underwater scene. Then, to welcome me, the wind kicked up a blinding cloud of gray silt, stinging my face and arms. The enduring barbed wire fence braced against the driving hot winds, its mile square enclosure dotted only by the tough sagebrush and the knee-high pyramid-shaped red ant hills.

As I walked past the front gate, I remembered the hostile white soldiers that stood ten feet tall at attention, their fixed bayonet-rifles at their sides. A tingle of fear ran through me. The landmarks, building foundations, concrete slabs, graveled roads, and open drainage ditches appeared smaller than I had remembered them in my faded mind's eye.

Relying on memory, I located the hospital grounds along the northern boundary, then the first row of Blocks 1 through 7. Each block consisted of a mess hall, latrines, and twelve Army barracks. There were six rows of seven blocks. From the northeast corner, Block 7, I counted back to Block 4, our block, to our old mess hall, the latrines, then where Building 10 used to be. The buildings were gone, sold to farmers for chicken coops and tool sheds. "Ain't fit for human use," one old timer told me later when I examined what he called his "barn," the main structure on his hog farm just outside of town. Only the half buried two by six frame of our front porch remained, marking the entranceway to our twenty by twenty foot one-room living quarters. Beside the porch, a monument of stones left behind during our hasty exit stood guard.

ABOVE: Toru, kneeling by the porch remains of Apartments C and D, Block 4, Building 10, Topaz concentration camp, 1995.

Those small stones jogged my memory of my old secret hiding place. Like a kid again, I was on all fours, exploring the front corner of our porch. I broke through the hard desert crust with a stone, then dug down elbow deep into the loose sand . . . and there huddled together and waiting was my childhood treasure. Twenty-six sparkling marbles! My boyhood gems, my most cherished possessions!

Stunned—I stopped . . . and remembered . . . I was five again . . . It was 1944 once more . . . the smell of the dry desert air awoke memories asleep almost a lifetime . . . I saw my pals, Arthur and Bobby, and my brother, Jiro, again in front of our barrack. There was a four-foot circle drawn on the ground and a pot of eight marbles clustered in the center. I was crouched on my knees behind the line; it was my turn to take aim and let my red agate "lucky shooter" fly, while the others watched closely that I didn't fudge. I heard the mess hall triangle begin to scream . . . and Mama's voice repeat, in her broken English, "Toru! Jiro! Washy hand, time to eat!!"

As Mama's voice faded . . . I remained kneeling on the scorching hot ground, the heat burning through my jeans. Gradually, I returned to the here and now. I realized the catastrophic results of that unjustified imprisonment, the psychological and emotional damage we had suffered and endured in silence throughout our lives. I felt a painful lump swell in my throat . . . my eyes watered, blurring the brilliantly colored marbles gleaming in my cupped hands.

Toru Saito

Toru Saito was born on December 11, 1937, in Japantown, San Francisco. As a five-year-old he was interned at Tanforan Racetrack, then Topaz concentration camp. At eight years old he was released, and he and his family moved to Hunter's Point, San Francisco, then later to Berkeley.

For twenty years, Toru worked as a mental health clinician at the City of Berkeley's Mental Health Clinic. His lifelong passions are music and gardening. Accompanied by guitar, he has sung publicly since 1955. In 1983, he formed "The Shanghai Bar" band, which plays Broadway standards from the 1930s and '40s. He serves as the official bandleader and singer.

Daisy Uyeda Satoda

Ganbare[1]
February 12, 1942 - Lincoln's Birthday

With badges flashing, the FBI swarm the house:

They strip bedding to the springs
Tear clothes from closets
Clear shelves of books
Scrutinize albums and scrapbooks
Denude walls of paper.

Agents seat Papa in a chair
In the middle of the kitchen
Where we cling to each other.
Mama silently follows them
From room to room.

Mitsuzo Uyeda now,
"Dangerous enemy alien."
Agents order Papa, "Get dressed.
We are taking you to the city jail
For further questioning."

Mama hands him an overnight bag
Packed with toiletries

ABOVE: Daisy Uyeda Satoda, 1944 and 2001.
OPPOSITE : Sunset, Topaz, Utah, c. 1943. Photo by K. Kido, Topaz Photo Studio.

The Uyeda family;
(top row) friend;
(middle) Kaye, Doris,
Roz, Don; (front)
Annabelle, Flo, and
Daisy (lower right).
Watsonville, Ca.
c. 1931.

And a change of clothing.
We sob and flail away
At agents who dangle handcuffs.

Marshall and Juneko call out,
"Papa!" "Papa!" "Paa-Paa!"
And grab him around the legs.
Mama bows to the man in charge.
He orders:

"No handcuffs. No shackles.
Do not humiliate this man.
He won't flee but flank him,
Just in case."
Head held high,

Papa turns
To his eleven children
And says,
"*Sayonara*. This parting is not forever.
We will be together again.

Ganbare!"

¹ *Ganbare* – To do your best.

❦

Tanforan Assembly Center

Family

In May of 1942, the bus arrived at the gates of Tanforan Racetrack in San Bruno, California. I was a bewildered 14-year-old who did not understand why we were being uprooted and sent to a camp. After a two-hour bus ride from Oakland, we were greeted at the barbed wire fence by a horde of Japanese faces whose smiles assured us that things were going to be okay. Passing through a phalanx of armed sentries, we were led to the processing center where we received our housing assignment. Our family was fortunate to be housed in Army-style barracks and not the filthy, smelly horse stables.

My mother received special dispensation to remain in Oakland for a few days, because she was totally exhausted from sewing clothes, packing, selling our furniture, and arranging for the storage of our personal belongings. Since my father had been arrested by the FBI and was not around, Mama became head of our household. When her nights of preparation without sleep caused her to collapse, my sister Flo was appointed to stay behind with her.

Since we were allowed to take only what we could carry, and we did not have enough luggage, Mama decided to sew large duffel bags. Our bags were extra heavy because she had wisely instructed us: "Stuff them as full as possible. The authorities said one bag each, but they did not put any limit on their size and weight."

Not knowing how long we would be gone, my mother talked the officials into allowing her to take our oversize professional sewing machine. "I need it. I have eleven children," she said to the military guard. Crossing her arms, she continued, "I'm sorry but I will not get on the bus without my machine." Because her short, fat body was blocking the bus entrance the officers acceded to her demands by promising to send the machine on a later bus.

My father had been arrested by the FBI as a so-called "dangerous" leader in the Japanese community and was being held incommunicado at the Immigration and Naturalization prison at Sharp Park in Pacifica. Earlier we had sent a letter of protest to the FBI and to Mrs. Eleanor Roosevelt, wife of President Franklin D. Roosevelt, asking for my father's release because of the hardship his detention was causing our large family. Flo was designated to write the letter because she was a college student, and we thought she was very bright. Flo wrote:

"Papa is our sole breadwinner and we have no other source of income. Also, our mother, at 50 years of age, has no marketable skills to support her eleven children, ranging in age from 21 down to 4 years. We are totally dependent on our father who is innocent of the charges lodged against him because an old man of 62 with 11 children has no time for extracurricular activities, let alone subversive ones."

The government must have felt compassion for our plight because, a few months later, my father shocked us by walking into our barracks. He was the first Issei to be paroled by the Justice Department. Totaling thirteen persons, we were officially listed as the largest intact family in Tanforan.

Our Barrack Home

I walked the long dirt-covered main road which led to our temporary home. The constant friction of my new grown-up beige $3.99 shoes produced several painful blisters. As we passed the barracks, a radio was playing popular tunes of the '40s: "I got spurs that Jingle Jangle, Jingle, as I go riding merrily along . . ." "A Sleepy Lagoon, a tropical moon . . ." These two songs became synonymous with Tanforan although there certainly were no spurs or lagoons here. All I saw were never-ending rows of tarpaper-covered barracks, hundreds of horse stables, the race-track, a grandstand where the bachelors slept, and community wide mess halls, latrines, and laundry rooms, plus a lot of Japanese people—8,000 of them.

I hated the twice daily head count. With barbed wire fences encircling our camp, where could we inmates possibly go? And I resented it when the barrack manager gave us thirteen white cotton bags. He instructed: "Stuff these bags with straw which is piled next to the stables. These bags will be your mattresses so place them on the metal cots in your room." The cots were the only furniture in our room. The straw mattresses and the dust caused my first case of hay fever, which triggered a lifetime of allergic reactions.

Friendships

The communal latrines had no curtains or doors and the toilets sat side by side, two to a compartment. The partitions were only shoulder high when we were seated. The showers were activated by pulling an overhead string, and we never knew whether we would get hot or cold water. Katy, May, Esther, Ruth, Nellie, and I took our showers in the afternoons when we had a better chance of getting warm water. We soon lost

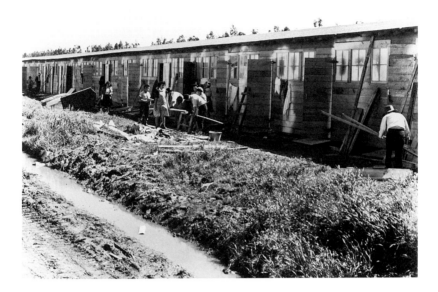

all modesty. We pranced around the shower room, singing and dancing in the nude. However, Chiz was very shy. She draped a towel over the shower enclosure for privacy and never joined in our bathroom revelry.

Although we thought we were carefree, in retrospect we must have been experiencing some underlying stress because the seven of us never had our menstrual periods during the five months we were in Tanforan. Actually we were relieved to have amenorrhea. It was too embarrassing to go down to the canteen to buy sanitary napkins since several of the boys we knew worked there. This condition was too delicate and personal to discuss with others outside our group. I now wonder if other teenagers had this problem.

Camp life was the beginning of my independence. Since it was not cool to eat with our parents in the mess hall, the seven of us ate our meals together. After each meal, we would dash off to the recreation hall where we spent all of our free time. The workers kept us busy with activities and sports. We formed a club for junior high school girls and called our-selves the Junior Miss. We had coed socials. Since my sister Rose and I knew how to jitterbug, we taught the other kids this popular dance. Even the adult leaders became our pupils.

ABOVE: April 29, 1942, Tanforan Assembly Center, San Bruno, Calif. Racetrack horse stalls are remodeled for family living quarters. Internees are building benches chairs, tables, and shelves for their belongings from scrap lumber. Barracks are equipped with only a bed and mattress for each person. Dorothea Lange, WRA photograph, National Archives at College Park.

Goodbye

By the end of summer, rumors started to circulate. We heard that prisoner-of-war camps were being erected throughout the country, and these would serve as our homes for the duration of the war. We knew the assembly centers were temporary holding areas, but we had no idea where we were going to be sent. We even heard that we might be shipped to Japan for hostage exchange.

Our last weeks in Tanforan were filled with despair because we knew we were going to be sent to some God-forsaken spot in the interior, and we prayed that we would not be separated and sent to different camps. Most of us had never traveled beyond the Bay Area. It was during the last days in Tanforan that my girl friends and I really said goodbye. As we stood at the barbed wire fence behind my barrack, looking out on El Camino Real Highway, we pressed our faces against the cold steel. We wistfully waved at each car as it whizzed past us until each one slowly receded into a speck.

The Bath

Mr. and Mrs. Kato were an elderly, childless Issei couple who lived in the end room of our barrack in Topaz. The block people thought the couple was strange because they always kept to themselves, never joining in the block's activities.

With her dark penciled eyebrows, bright red lipstick, and face sprinkled liberally with white powder, Mrs. Kato was the caricature of a Japanese clown. Her hair was dyed jet black with ringlets that framed her rouged face. She wore party dresses of satin and velvet along with her gold kid slippers. Mrs. Kato kept a large blond-tressed doll on her bed, and she often sat outside her barrack, cradling the doll in her arms, and crooning to it in Japanese.

Mr. Kato had vitiligo, a skin condition characterized by large patches of white unpigmented areas on his brown face. He resembled a lemur with the same ghostly appearance. My girl friend Etchie and I thought he had some incurable, contagious disease, and we made sure he never touched us. We tried to avoid him as he smiled and muttered unintelligible Japanese words that sounded very nasty.

Mr. Kato always wore a *yukata* (a cotton kimono) and *geta* (bath clogs) on his way to the washroom. He bathed during the day when we were gabbing on my porch. Mr. Kato made a pretense of keeping his *yukata* closed as he toted his personal wash basin which held his bathing supplies. He leered at us with his toothless grin and made feeble attempts to hold his *yukata* together when the wind blew it open, exposing his dried up genitalia. After witnessing several accidental exposures, Etchie and I would run into my room whenever we saw old man Kato heading for the bathroom. He offered us candy, cheap costume jewelry, and occasionally waved a $5 bill at us which Etchie was tempted to take.

Etchie was a naive 14-year-old whose mother had recently died in a sanitarium. Consequently there was no mother figure to tell her about the "facts of life." I was an older 15-year-old who was just as ignorant about sex. However, our 12-year-old friend June warned us to stay away from the old man whispering, "Etchie could get pregnant if Mr. Kato ever poked her in the side with a pencil!"

In our block of 300 people, the Issei men requested two of the four communal bathtubs which were assigned to the women since they were accustomed to soaking in hot tub water and only had showers on their side of the washroom. After a long argument at a block meeting, the women reluctantly agreed to give up one bathtub, which was then partitioned off to open up into the men's shower room. For some reason, the partition did not reach the floor.

One day everyone near the washrooms was startled to hear my father's voice yell out, "*Baka yaro! Nani o shiteru no ka?* (You fool! What are you doing?)" My father had caught Mr. Kato pouring water onto the floor. Mr. Kato had evidently filled up his wash basin repeatedly with water from his tub and sloshed it toward the adjoining women's cubicle. He hoped to create a reflection that would capture the image of the women's bottoms as they unknowingly stepped in and out of the tub. Mr. Kato frantically started to drain the water while gathering up his bathing supplies to make a quick exit.

The men had frequently complained that Kato took too much time while taking a bath, and several men ran from the showers to see what the commotion was about. When Papa told the men what Kato was doing, they grabbed the old man, cowering by the side of his tub, and threw him on the floor. Then they shoved him out the door, naked, into the freezing snow. Several men yelled out in Japanese at Kato's retreating back, "We will give you a real beating if we catch you again." Later I heard some men laughing, and they said the old man was so frightened that his entire face turned white and you could not see where his vitiligo began or ended.

Our block, like the rest of the camp, had its own justice system. At a specially-convened block meeting, the outraged women, as well as us teenage girls, demanded action in banning Kato from using the men's bathtub. Mr. Kato was too ashamed to attend the meeting.

Mr. Kato stayed in his barrack room after the incident, and Mrs. Kato had to brave the stares of the angry block people as she took home their meals from the mess hall. The night watchman told my father that thereafter Kato went to the washroom after 2:00 a.m. to take his showers because no one bathed that late at night.

The next month the couple left Topaz without saying goodbye to anyone.

❦

Segregation and the Loyalty Questionnaire
Topaz, Utah Concentration Camp

Like all children under the age of 17, I did not have to answer the loyalty questionnaire in February of 1943. However, those adults who replied "No" to both questions #27 and #28 were considered "disloyal" and shipped in September to a high-security segregation center at Tule Lake in Northern California. The innocent victims of the segregation movement were the minor children of those "No-No" adults who chose to go to Tule Lake. They were our classmates and our playmates who had no voice in the questionnaire but were forced to leave their friends behind to accompany their parents.

One boy in my class, Minoru, refused to go to Tule Lake with his family. He was declared an emancipated minor and given quarters at the Administration housing building where he worked as a maintenance assistant. He was only 15 years old and classmates teased him about his "sissiness" because he was thought to be gay. Bright and articulate, he often referred to the Constitution in the classroom. "As an American citizen my civil rights are being violated," he would state. "We are all being held illegally behind barbed wire." The rest of us giggled nervously because we were too frightened to challenge anything that formidable. Those remaining years in Topaz must have been very lonely for him because he did not have any relatives or friends whom he could depend on for guidance or support.

The upheaval created by the segregation program added another unhappiness to our young lives. We had to say goodbye to our best buddies. We wept when they left Topaz, thinking that we would never see them again. The ever-present grapevine rumored they were to be sent to Japan or to "real" concentration camps.

Within a month after we had said goodbye to our old friends, a new group of students were sent from Tule Lake to continue their life of incarceration in Topaz. We were wary of these new teenagers who were the children of families who had answered "Yes-Yes." These people were from the Sacramento area, as well as Oregon and Washington. Their clothing style differed from ours. The girls wore short, white trench coats, clogs, and colored bobby socks. The guys wore baggy jeans that were not Levis. The girls lifted their hair in big pompadours, and the boys had short haircuts. We noticed the Northerners had just a trace of a Japanese accent whereas the Bay Area kids had more noticeable accents. Of course, our new classmates were not happy to be uprooted for the third time in one year, leave their friends behind in Tule Lake, and move to a new camp filled with strangers who were unfriendly to them. Initially, they formed their own cliques and kept to themselves.

In time we did recover from the separation from our old friends. We eventually welcomed the new arrivals by encouraging them to take part in school activities, such as running for class and school offices, joining the various clubs, committees, and sports teams. As a matter of fact, a lot of the Tuleans turned out to be the sports stars of Topaz High. After we got over our suspicions, we started to run around with new friends who had funny names like Bubbles, Wyno, Starr, Kiko, Wiichi, Tomato, Jaxon, and Wasco. They soon joined up with our equally comically-named teenagers, including Wacky, King Tut, Ratcho, Spider, Potay, Joker, Jiggs, Dorsey, Tugboat, Zombie, and Beau Jack.

Throughout all the controversy of the loyalty questionnaire and our changing friendships, one thing remained constant for the duration of our three years' stay in Topaz: our living conditions were deplorable. We suffered through the sandstorms that pelted our faces like shards of glass and the dust storms that seeped through the windows and doors of our living quarters, which left endless blankets of white, talc-like powder on our floors and furniture. We suffered though the long walk to school in extreme, inclement weather, the lousy food, education without a school-house, shared books, and an uncertified faculty that left most of us unqualified for college. We suffered through the constant ritual of lining up for our meals, fighting for washtubs in the laundry room, the shared latrines, the lines at the co-op whenever some hard-to-get items were received. And, most of all, we suffered through the nagging feeling that no one in America gave a damn about us.

In spite of these adversities, all of us came through with a good sense of self because of our indomitable *Yamato damashii* (Japanese spirit) whereby our parents taught us to live by such words and phrases as *ganbare* (tenacity), *giri* (duty), *on* (obligation), and *gaman* (tolerance). Without this upbringing, we would not have been able to cope with the physical hardships, extreme weather conditions, inadequate education, loss of friends, the upheaval of our personal lives, and the endless uncertainties created by our wartime imprisonment.

❦

Topaz, 1993

Ghosts from a distant past lay buried in these desert sands
    Where we return to retrace the saga of our youth.
Three tumultuous years stripped us of innocence.
    We were banished behind barbed wire,
Held captive in this one-mile square:
    Topaz, "Jewel of the Desert."

Greasewood bushes, giant anthills, and rotted sewers
    Replace the barracks, guard towers, and latrines.
No evidence remains: not of Topaz,
    The blistering heat of summer, the biting cold of winter;
Not of savage sandstorms
    Which sifted through the walls and windows.

Happy times are evoked in our remembrances.
    Again we jitterbug to the Big Bands.
Our ears are glued to the radio, to top songs from the Hit Parade.
    Though a faceless future loomed before us,
We still dared to dream
    About a life beyond the gates of our exile.

Fifty years later we return to this wasteland, our children
    Unable to fathom that there is nothing here,
No vestige that we existed.
    Our past has disappeared. Did it never happen?
Our return to Topaz after half a century
    Is a trek to bury our ghosts.

Our children cannot believe there was life in Topaz.
    They search and dig but unearth no reminders of our youth.

This barren land belies our years of infamy.
    They will find no legacies, just shadows of a bygone era.
To them, Topaz is a time and not a place.
    But to us, Topaz will remain forever.

Daisy Uyeda Satoda

From 1942 to 1945, Daisy Uyeda Satoda spent her high school years in a concentration camp at Topaz, Utah. She is a seventy-three-year-old Sansei who is continuing her education in the Humanities department at San Francisco State University. Daisy enjoys volunteering her time with several local and national Japanese American organizations. She is involved with program planning, fundraising, and volunteer recruitment. She has also been active with the organization of the various reunions of her Topaz High class of 1945 as well as the all-Topaz camp gatherings.

Ms. Satoda is grateful to the California Civil Liberties Public Education Program for recognizing the importance of recording the personal stories of life behind barbed wire in one of the most shameful chapters of American history. The unparalleled stories of this experience have been locked up in the minds and hearts of former internees for almost sixty years. The Internment Autobiography Writing Workshop, led by Brian Komei Dempster, has provided the opportunity for Daisy and others to recall the bittersweet memories of their incarceration.

ABOVE: Foundation block of washroom/latrine. Topaz, Utah, 1993. Photograph by Tak Yamamoto.

Harumi Serata

❧

Seatoru no Ojisan
(Old Man from Seattle)
Story from Minidoka

Walking to school, we would notice an old man standing by the main road, his suitcase beside him. He wore an overcoat and hat. He was short and had the neglected look of a bachelor in his rumpled clothes. After school he was still there and stayed until it became dark. Day after day, the old man stood by the road in the heat and dust. People began to bring him food and water. "*Dozo haitte kudasai* (Please come inside)," they pleaded.

"This must be a mistake," Seattle Ojisan said. "I live in Seattle and must be lost. I must return to my home in Seattle." He would go to the Administration to complain, and he became a nuisance. "The bus will be coming soon," they told him. "Be ready."

I can't remember how long he stood by the road, hunched over in the blazing desert sun. He looked so tired, disoriented, and discouraged from waiting so long.

One day he was gone. Other people said he had returned to Seattle, but Mom told me, "Ojisan was sent to Steilacoom Mental Hospital in Washington."

ABOVE: Harumi Serata, 1941 and 2001.
OPPOSITE: "I was the May Day Queen in the 6th grade." Harumi (center) wearing white dress and cape with train, 1941. Minidoka Relocation Center.

Obake Obasan
(Ghostly Lady)

There was a lady in camp who wore pale makeup and had long flowing hair. "She looks like an *obake*," Mama said. She was slender and demure but her face was sad with its pair of downcast eyes. In public, she hardly smiled or laughed. She walked gracefully and may have had training as a dancer. She played the *shamisen* (string instrument) and spoke Japanese beautifully.

Although she never married, she had a daughter who attended college on the East Coast and would visit her mother during the summer break. She was rather plain, stocky, and not graceful like her mother. She loved her mother but was embarrassed by her fragile condition and would be overprotective, often speaking for her.

My friend's mother and Obasan were close. They were both single mothers who enjoyed making paper flowers. When I was selected May Day queen, she made me a crown of paper roses and they looked almost real. I remember going to her room where she greeted me, dressed in her long silk kimono robe. She fussed over me, patting my hair. "*Totemo kawaii* (Very pretty)," she said.

I still don't know about her past or how she came to America. There were rumors she was a geisha. Our mothers would whisper about her, but we were never told the real story. She might have come as a picture bride and found herself betrayed. Whoever she really was, she did not have an easy life. In those days, life was harsh to a woman who did not have a man.

Bitter Brush Story

On our block the Issei men would walk into the desert, searching for bitter brush branches with unusual shapes. They would gleefully compare the branches and imagine what figures they saw. "Those men are acting like children," Mama said. The branches would be polished into a sheen and shaped into cranes, snakes, birds, and other animals. Mr. Konishi, who was particularly enthusiastic about his new hobby, would walk far into the desert looking for just the right branches.

When winter came and the weather turned cold, most of the men stopped going into the desert, but Mr. Konishi went by himself. He enjoyed the solitude of being alone to appreciate the beauty of the snow. "*Korewa watakushi no tanoshimi* (This is my pleasure)," he would say.

One day Mr. Konishi did not return from his walk. The sky was turning dark and his wife feared the worst. "*Iwao mada kaette nai* (My husband has not come home)," she said. "Please help me." The men on our block quickly formed a search group and went into the desert looking for Mr. Konishi. They searched several days before he was found, his body covered with snow where he had frozen to death. Unable to stay awake, he lay down and fell asleep beside a bitter brush bush. They discovered him less than a mile from camp. He probably could not see the lights and became lost without a compass.

A gloom fell over the block, and some men blamed themselves. "I should have gone with him," they said. Enthusiasm for the bitter brush figurines waned, each branch a reminder of what happened to Mr. Konishi. Finally the group disbanded. It wasn't enjoyable anymore.

ABOVE : Harumi (circled) 5th grade class, Minidoka Relocation Center, 1943.

❦

Fortune Telling

We sat around a card table with only three legs. We did not unfold the fourth leg and this gave the table an uneven balance. We put our fingers lightly on the edge of the table and asked various questions. "Does Johnny like me? Will he ask me out?" Then we said, "Knock once for yes and twice for no." The table would dip once or twice most of the time. One of the frequently asked questions was: "How much longer will the war last?" The table dipped twice, once for each year.

One day we decided to dim the lights, light candles, and pull down the shades. It was like a séance. When we asked our questions the table did a deep dip, and we heard a noise like a knock. We screamed and turned on the lights. Everyone swore they did not push the table.

We didn't play Fortune Telling after that, and we always kept the lights on.

ABOVE: Harumi describes her 5th grade class, Minidoka Relocation Center: "The pupils look so obedient with their hands folded. A small figurine on the table takes away the starkness of the room. No one is smiling, and I wonder why. Were we being staged to show how well we were being treated? I remember the photographer was a white man, and the teacher wanted us to make a good impression. I don't know why, but the photographer might have been an inspector conducting an evaluation.

The tables and chairs were hastily constructed with two by four lumber. We really didn't have books or reading materials. Miss Erickson, our teacher, was from the Midwest. She was very strict, prim, and proper. She did not have contact with Japanese people before, and it must have been difficult to teach under these conditions in camp.

School in camp was my great joy. Friendships were developed that made camp life bearable. We were all equals in the same situation. School took away the boredom, but I can't say we studied very hard. We did not have current books and when I returned to Fife, Washington, I was way behind the other children and had to work hard to catch up."

Rumors

Some Issei believed we would be liberated from camp by the Japanese Army. They would report sightings of Japanese soldiers on the streets. "How stupid," Mama said. "They are probably American soldiers with Asian faces."

Rumors periodically circulated about Japanese forces landing and making their way to the camps. "We must be strong and *gaman* (persevere)," Mama's friend would whisper. "We will be free soon." Mama felt sad because of her friend's ignorance.

When the Japanese government sent shoyu and miso to us through the Red Cross, it only affirmed to Mama's friend that we were not forgotten. It tasted so good, and we ate it sparingly in our own room.

Mama's friend made an emergency trip to Salt Lake City and came to visit upon her return. In a whisper she reported, "The Japanese soldiers are now stationed in Salt Lake City. I saw the *hino-maru* (Japanese flag) flying over their headquarters." Mama was stunned. "Can this be true, she saw it with her own eyes?" Word came later from people in Salt Lake City that what she had seen was the Red Cross flag flying over their building. "How stupid," Mama said.

Why did these people have this fantasy of being rescued? I can only speculate it was because they felt abandoned and betrayed by the government that had imprisoned them.

Ghost Story

After returning to Fife, Papa worked a variety of hard labor jobs, including repairing railroad tracks, cleaning out ditches, and working on the farms. Finally he accepted a job at the oyster farm in South Bend, Washington, near the ocean, over 100 miles from Fife. Papa hauled in the oysters from the cold water, and Mama worked at the plant shucking the oysters. Papa had to work according to the tide, and Mama did piecework. Luckily, they had a truck to commute and came home on the weekends.

They were assigned to live in a company house a few miles away. The house was abandoned for years and very dirty with stained tissues on the floor. Mama said there was an old bed, stove, table and chairs, but not much else. Transients had used it as a crash pad, and lovers also used it as a boudoir.

Soon after Mama and Papa moved in, they experienced shadows and noises, but they ignored them since they needed the job. Mama complained to Papa, but he told her, "It's not going to be forever. *Gaman* (persevere)." People at the oyster farm asked, "Are you alright living at the house? Most people don't stay there very long." No one used the word haunted.

One night, Papa had to work since the tide was out, and Mama was there alone. Suddenly the lights went out. "I struggled to light the kerosene lamp," she said, "but after it was lit, a strong gust of wind inside the house blew it out. Each time I relit the lamp it was blown out and I was afraid. I realized it was not natural and the house was haunted. I had only a small light from the wood-burning kitchen stove which cast an eerie shadow on the wall. The wind howled through the house. The ghosts were most mischievous in trying to drive me out. They wanted the house for themselves."

When Papa came back, Mama hysterically said, "I will not spend another day in this house." The next day he drove her home to Fife.

We didn't believe Mama or the ghost story. We thought she just didn't like the house and working at the oyster farm. Papa said, "You are being silly and letting me down." He returned to the oyster job alone but came home a short time later since it was a seasonal job.

Mama and Papa did not talk about this experience much, and after a while it wasn't mentioned at all except when we ate those small Olympia oysters. They were so delicious and fresh we ate them raw. Mama and Papa also brought home clams cooked in shoyu. They were small, soft but still chewy, with a wonderful flavor like abalone.

Years later, when Papa was an old man, I mentioned to him the time Mama came home, complaining about the ghosts. I thought Papa would chuckle, but instead he frowned and said, "It was true. The house was haunted. I still remember the many nights I slept in the truck." "Why did you stay?" I asked. He replied, "I needed the job and had a family to feed."

History II

The War is History.
We are living in the future.
We are driving Toyota cars

and watching Sony TVs.
We visit Japan and even
speak their language.

Have we forgiven them?
It is hard to tell since we have
the face of the enemy.

Harumi Serata
Harumi Serata was born and raised in Tacoma, Washington, in the suburb of Fife. She was interned with her family in Minidoka, Idaho. Retired from State service, she now volunteers at various nonprofit agencies. She was recipient of the Kay Okamoto Volunteer Award in 1997. She is married to Walter Kenbo Serata and lives in San Francisco. She has written extensively about her family history. "If their story is not written, they will be forgotten," she says.

Michi Tashiro

Transformation of a Rice Sack

"*Aiii . . . do desu, what dis?*" cried Badger as she sat on a small stool, dangling her short legs. Her toes barely brushed against the coarse wooden floor. While fidgeting her bottom into the bowl of the seat, her body lurched forward, and she flung her right foot onto the far end of a square grilled metal treadle. When the plate began to teeter-totter like a see-saw, Badger quickly threw her left foot on the near edge of the plate to balance the totter of the teeter. "*Ah, so desu, dis how to do.*"

Ka-chan, ka-chan, groaned the machine.

While furiously working the pedal, her pudgy hands tensely held the edge of the rice sack that lay before her and hesitantly guided it forward. The rose design on the cloth began to shimmy and shake, then unexplainably crept to the table's edge. Badger lost her grip, and the rice sack slid off the table, sending a flutter of red rose petals onto her lap. "*Shaku!*" She pursed her fat lips, picked up the sacking and flung it back onto the table. "*Eh, komatta yo* (what a fix)."

"I do ebi-ting like Yott-chan *Sensei* say—draw good line . . . make neat edge, use straight edge ru-ra . . . hold together wid pin, no *sko-chi te-pu* (Scotch tape)." While realigning the material on the table, Badger recalled the easy 1-2-3 steps drilled into her by Yott-chan, her sewing teacher. "Maybe ru-ra not straight, *hasami* (scissors) not sharp, hundred pound *kome* rice sack too big . . . I don' know. Yott-chan . . . *shinsetsu* (so kind) . . . she tell me how one more time. Maybe I study myself . . .

ABOVE: Michi Tashiro, 1945 and 1999.
OPPOSITE: Michi's mother, Yukino Tashiro, 1938, b. Oct. 20, 1895 – d. Dec. 4, 1987. Photo by George Tashiro.

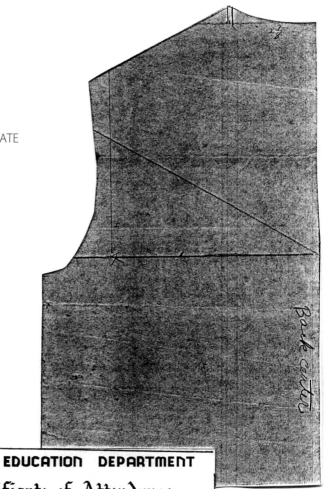

DRAFTING CERTIFICATE
MAY 3, 1945

DRAFTED PATTERN
(On brown paper)

Yukino Tashiro
11E 8E
Amache, Colorado
1942-1945

in book she gib me." When the fabric finally lay flat and still, Badger made a few more stitches.

Ka-cha, ka-cha . . . ping!

"What dat? Oh, t'read broke . . . " She pushed herself away from the table, exasperated, then wiped sweat from her brow. She readjusted the tortoise shell comb that had worked its way out of her hair bun. She had half a notion to hustle over to the Camp Co-op store, which was just kitty-corner across the open athletic field from her place, 11E-8E, and get a few notions—a spool of thread, new needle, and perhaps a little seam binding. She scratched her head, then leaned over to root around in her sewing basket.

"I like 'Clark' t'read . . . cotton . . . strong. Maybe Matsuoka-san, head store man, hab some." Such materials were hard to come by because of the War, and even Yoshiko *Sensei* had to catalogue-order supplies for her sewing class. "Awww . . . Matsuoka-san, he a'ways say, 'ratso shuz (lots of shoes), but no t'read. All dat kind t'ing—string, rope, t'read—An ko Sam make into net . . . you know . . . to ka-ba up big gun. Bettah I order from Denber." The Denver Post Household Arts Department was Badger's favorite order place, and, being the closest big city to Camp Amache, it often came through with the goods. "Hah, I got." Her fingers grasped a spool of white mercerized cotton thread—extra heavy duty, the good stuff that she brought with her to Camp. "Bettah, now no go see Matsuoka-san . . . too hot . . . no shade, burning sand . . ." She sighed, threaded the needle, and resumed pushing the treadle.

Ka-cha, ka-cha, ka-cha . . . !

With her eagle eye she drew straight lines, cut straight edges, stitched straight seams, just like Yott-chan taught her. But the darts were not pointed, the pleats wouldn't stay pleated, and the ruffles ruffled her feathers all the while that she was sewing. "*Namu Ami . . . namu Ami,*" she intoned, asking for Buddha's guiding hand and thankful that Crane wasn't nearby nagging. "Good dat Crane at work . . . not here. He a'ways telling me how to do . . . like I no can learn myself. But he sure good cook . . . e-ben make pork'n bean taste sweet like *azuki* (red beans)." Most every day, Crane baked pies and sweets in the hospital kitchen and in Block 11E mess hall—for only $16 a month.

"It OK . . . he mess in mess hall . . . not at home. 'Hold sack tighter . . . put stick higher . . . draw circle rounder . . . pin ob'er there, not here

. . . and don' push down feet so hard,' he say. I no hear him, 'cause dis like driving old car . . . put feet down hard, go straight . . . not so hard, den go zigzag like drunk farmer running t'rough rice paddy. *Aii* . . . *urusai* (he's pesty) . . . I t'ink so." She switched the material to the other side of the machine and the rose bud danced across the tabletop.

After the final seam was sewn, she undid her new creation from the machine, bit off loose thread with her eyetooth and placed the clothing on the cot nearby. "*Ah, mo sunda*, all t'rough," she said, rubbing her sore legs, dog tired. Suddenly realizing the lateness of the day, she squirmed off the stool, hurriedly wrapped the garment around her waist, and hustled off to do the early shift at the mess hall. She bussed some US issue silverware off the table into the pocket of her new outfit, and brushed crumbs from its skirt. Then glancing down at its bib, Badger proudly proclaimed to her fellow KPers, "Dis kroz (clothes) good for wiping hand . . . keep warm when cold . . . no mess on *kimono*. But best, it got b-i-i-i-g pocket."

"Oh . . . red rose right in front . . . I sew pretty good, *neh*? Yott-chan be proud of me . . . I make perfect 'Cal Rose' rice sack apron!"

Epilogue:

Badger, *tanuki*, in Japanese lore, can transform from beast to human and back again, at will. This magical power is used judiciously to accomplish amazing, yet often baffling, deeds as man and mischievously trick its adversary as a badger. My mother was indeed, the incarnate Badger. After the War, the family resettled in San Francisco, where Badger, garbed in her "Cal Rose" rice sack apron, tucked in many a ball gown seam for the matrons of Pacific Heights.

Crane, *tsuru*, signifies happiness and long life, both of which my father achieved after many years of hard work. His innovative mind led him eventually to attach a motor to Mom's treadle sewing machine. Years later, when Mom turned deaf to his constant kibbitzing, Dad scooted onto the stool himself, revved the Singer, and re-upholstered all the living room furniture. I will always remember him as the weathered laborer turned crafty artisan. He was a silent man, except when he yelled at Badger about how to do things.

Yoshiko, one of 50 internee teachers in Camp Amache, was probably younger than Mom; therefore, she was endearingly called "*Yott-chan*."

The Singer was traded in for a new model in the 1970s.

❦

The Picnic

With *onigiri* (rice balls) in hand, we sneaked out under the barbed wire fence to picnic on the biggest sun-baked sand hill we could find—just out of eyesight of the guard in his tower. The sun was so hot that the rattlers, considerably wiser than us, stayed home in their cool burrows under the rocks, the sage, and the cactus. But before brother, sister, or I could spread out our goodies for lunch, the sky darkened, fire ants scurried out from their sand hill digs, and dirt devils scooted about in ever widening circles over the desert floor. On the horizon a sand funnel emerged. It joined the dancing dirt devils and ominously swayed in a rumba toward us.

Hot sand flew into our faces, blurred our vision, and covered the *onigiri* like a generous sprinkling of *goma* (sesame seeds). Grit, grit, grit, we thought, as we munched and ground sand between our teeth. "Ants!" I shouted as red and black critters crawled up our legs. We hopped about, brushing them away, and stomping on them. "Ants in your pants, ants in your pants," taunted brother. He laughed and whacked at our legs and the giant ants. With the aid of a gust of wind, I pushed brother into a bed of thorny cactus. "Ouch!" he yelped.

We froze momentarily, then realizing our picnic could not continue, threw our *onigiri* to the wind, scrambled back under the barbed wire fence for home—11E-8E—only a step ahead of the fury.  Once inside, we slammed the door shut and screamed at Papa and Mama, "Sandstorm!" Papa dropped a half-woven cigarette case he was working on and rushed over to the window. He sealed it as best he could. Mama helped by cramming sheets, blankets, paper, bits of this and pieces of that into every crevice, knothole, and gap in the wall. But when the storm hit, the sand *pock-pocked* on the rooftop and fine desert silt came flowing under the door, around the windows, through every pore of the black tarpaper. It blew across the floor, piling up like an anthill against the opposite wall.

Papa returned to his workbench and his weaving to await the passing of the storm. Mama followed close behind him, and, when Papa wasn't looking, she snitched a pair of tweezers from his toolbox. Brother had to pull down his pants, so Mama could pluck the fine hair-like stickers from his behind. Sister and I guffawed when he stooped over like a porcupine with its quills on alert. Afterwards, Mama took a bottle of iodine off the shelf behind the stove, and liberally slathered it over our

ant bites . . . and brother's behind. Mama always used iodine externally, and cod liver oil internally, regardless of our ailments. Whether the stinging was from our injuries or the treatment or the scolding, we howled louder than the raging storm outside.

We coughed and gasped in the crowded one-room hot box for a long while. We cursed the sand, the wind, the sun, and the ants. "Scary storm," cried sister. Brother looked at me and bristled, "All your fault . . . picking an anthill, what a deal, huh?" I shot back, "Hey, that was the only clear spot in them bushes." Then I shoved him. We were prisoners penned up too long. Our anger finally turned from the elements toward one another, until we nearly came to blows.

Unable to abide our cacophonous bickering any longer, Papa exploded, "*Got-ten* (goddamn)! *Bachi* (What goes around comes around)!" Then he gave us hell for crossing over the barbed wire fencing.

Eventually the wind stopped blowing, the once shifting sand lay quiet, and our clamoring subsided. Papa, always busy with his hands, laid down his nearly completed case, leaned over behind the stove into the storage space, and pulled out a forked, rattler-snarer stick—more beautiful, more intricate than a Calder sculpture. He grabbed some rope, his homemade wire cage, and he headed for the door.

"Sun hide . . . get cool . . . snake come out . . . I catch," he said. We all jumped up and followed him outside to watch the master at work. He was the damned best trapper in all of Camp Amache. Well, in Block 11E for sure. Being from the school of "do as I say, not as I do," Papa shouted, "Barb wire . . . danger . . . no come . . . go home, NOW!" He wildly shook the cage and stick at us, and we tripped over some

ABOVE: The Tashiro family's barrack, 11E–8E & 8F, Amache, Colorado. Watercolor by Yukino Tashiro, 1945.

sun-bleached driftwood. We ambled back through the tumbleweeds for home once again. From the stoop, we spied Papa lifting a section of the fencing, then squeeze through to the other side, and stealthily walk toward our picnic hill near the big snake's lair.

We stomped back into the house. Mama sensed our disappointment about our disrupted picnic and aborted snake hunt. In order to stifle our raucous discontent, she reached around the stove for the *tatami* (bamboo mat) and spread it over the sandy heap in the corner of the room. Then she pulled out her *jubako* (lunch box). From the shelf, where she kept her stash of mess hall leftovers, Mama took down a bowl of rice, and with some *umeboshi* (pickled plum) that she had preserved in a big glass jar, she made *umeboshi onigiri* (rice ball stuffed with pickled plum).

She placed these in the *jubako*, then we relished the tartness of *umeboshi* and drank tepid KOOL AID—no ice, of course. If we were older, Mama would have served her *umeshu* (plum wine), which she made with Papa's homemade whiskey and some *ume*. In spite of the velvety smoothness of a sip of *umeshu*, we thought, who cared—our favorite flavor. We bit, we sipped, then wiped dirt off our faces with our sleeves, ravenously devouring Mama's special *bento* (lunch).

When all was eaten, Mama wiped the empty *jubako* with a damp cloth, gently rubbing its peeling chipped corners. She tightly wrapped the box in her somber olive green and purple *furoshiki* (bundling cloth), which she stored in Papa's wooden box behind the stove. When we heard Papa coming home, we rushed to open the door. His lip moved, and snatches of *Kimigayo*, the Japanese anthem, went floating across the cooling heat waves. He had a successful hunt . . . he snagged two rattlers.

Mama eyed the snakes. "Papa skin snake," she said. "Dry meat . . . make medicine." "Yuk," we three replied. "No touch . . . if bite, iodine . . . cod libber oil . . . no good," Mama admonished. "Only snake medicine work," she threatened. She picked up a broom, swept anthill mounds from the foot of the potbelly, and swished them out the door.

Michi Tashiro

Born a farmer's daughter, Michi Tashiro grew up in the big town of Turlock, California, until the bomb fell on Pearl Harbor in 1941. Along with her parents and nine siblings, she was sent to Camp Amache, Colorado, where she stayed for three years. She returned to Cortez, California, after World War II ended in 1945. But life on the farm was not easy, so her family moved to San Francisco, where she has lived ever since. After working for the State of California for many years, she is ready for retirement. She hopes to spend her retirement years climbing every hill in the City and writing family stories.

Lesson Plans

❧

The Internment Autobiography Writing Workshop

Overview

The Internment Autobiography Writing Workshop described through-out this book was held at the Japanese Cultural & Community Center of Northern California from February 1999 to July of 2000. The bulk of the students' writings were generated in the first twelve months, when we met regularly for sessions of two hours. I ran this portion of the course primarily as a writing workshop in which students shared their work and received constructive feedback from me and their peers. Students balanced their time between the creation of new work and the revision of other pieces. Since February of 2000, we have shifted our emphasis, dedicating our efforts to producing this book.

I. Workshop Philosophy and Structure

From the very beginning, I knew the class would need to have some sort of organized writing structure. I chose chronology so each student could trace his or her emotional and psychological transformation during the years of their internment. Initially, I planned only six lessons, each of them based upon one of the major events of the Japanese American wartime experience: Pearl Harbor (Lesson 1); Arrival (Lesson 3); The Loyalty Questionnaire (Lesson 10); Departure from Camp (Lesson 11); Resettlement (Lesson 12); Redress (Lesson 14).

While these subjects were of great importance, I encouraged the students to infuse any given historical moment with their individual

OPPOSITE: Quilt by Naoko Yoshimura Ito, "Letting Go," fabric. Description and artist's biography, next page.

voices, to imprint it with their unique fingerprints. Freed up by the groundwork laid down by internment studies such as Michi Weglyn's *Years of Infamy*, and oral history collections such as John Tateishi's *And Justice For All*, our primary goal was not to be historians; instead each student could focus on memoir and other creative forms as vehicles to write his or her personalized version of the World War II internment experience.

Although familiar images such as barbed wire, freight trains, and guard towers remained crucial in the students' stories, I challenged them to explore other symbols, settings, and images which could convey the realities of camp life. For example, Lesson 2 (Lost Possessions) asked each student to write about an object his or her family lost during the war. Lesson 5 (Interpreting Photographs) asked each student to respond

Letting Go:
a quilt by Naoko Yoshimura Ito

This quilt, "Letting Go," is about an incident that happened while we were at Heart Mountain War Relocation Center. It is a metaphor of my own imprisoned teenage years.

Because of my Japanese ancestry, I was incarcerated at Heart Mountain during World War II at the age of fifteen. We could take only what we could carry, which meant we could not take pets. One day in camp, my brother and I found a small bird and captured it. Soon after we had Father make a cage for it. For one week, we noticed that the mother bird, fighting her fear of humans, brought her baby bird a worm each day. Since we could no longer stand separating the mother and baby, we let our pet go.

Naoko Yoshimura Ito
Naoko Yoshimura Ito was born in 1926 in San Francisco and lived there until 1942-1945 when she was incarcerated at Heart Mountain War Relocation Center in Wyoming, where she graduated from high school.

She has been actively involved in the quilting world for over twenty years. She was charter member of the East Bay Heritage Quilters and co-chaired their first Quilting Symposium in 1984 at Mills College in Oakland, California, and again in 1988. In 1986, she coordinated the first United States/Japan Quilting Symposium in Tokyo and Kyoto, Japan. Since then she has introduced many quilting teachers to Japan.

to a camp-related photograph. These were variations of assignments I had used previously in other workshops, tailored to the particular needs and goals of this group.

II. The Creative Process

During our class meetings, I emphasized freewriting as a tool for each student to develop his or her unique voice, style, and story. The writing prompts I gave them were specific and based upon whatever lesson plan I had created for any given class. Some exercises, for example, asked students to respond to a significant historical event or a certain theme; others encouraged them to write about a particular image or object.

"Keep your hand moving at all times," I exhorted them as they put pen to paper. "Don't censor out any thoughts." To encourage spontaneity, we did this activity as a group. The process of freewriting was liberating for the students because they did not feel burdened by high expectations. At the end of each ten to fifteen minute writing session, the students read their drafts aloud to the others, who often nodded their heads and smiled and chuckled in recognition. Some pieces inspired us to give the author a round of applause. A few pieces stunned us into silence or brought us to tears.

In conjunction with in-class freewrites, students were encouraged to keep a journal and write in it as much as they could. To accommodate the exciting but unpredictable nature of the creative process, my students and I found it useful to maintain a flexible approach toward their work. Although I placed a premium on the constant generation of new material, I did not want students to feel pressured to complete every single assignment. Driven by their passions for a particular subject, a student might work on a certain piece for weeks. At other times a student might struggle with a new topic and would refocus his or her energies toward revising their other work.

Sometimes I used excerpts from professional writers—such as Garrett Hongo, Joy Kogawa, David Mura, John Okada, James Mitsui, and Mitsuye Yamada—to illustrate a point or strategy and provide a springboard for students to develop their own ideas. For Lesson 10 (The Loyalty Questionnaire), I read aloud a short excerpt of *No-No Boy* by Okada. We discussed the plight of the main character, Ichiro, who is treated as a pariah by the postwar Japanese American community after answering "no" to the controversial loyalty questions 27 and 28, which asked all interned Japanese Americans of draft age to serve America during the war. For Lesson 13 (Silence), we looked at a brief passage from Kogawa's *Obasan*, a novel which explores the Japanese Canadian camp experience. Naomi Nakane, the main character, examines the silence of the older generation, represented by the character of Obasan.

Many types of exchange and transformation took place as we grew into a tightly knit community, bonded by the common goal to uncover the past. Just as my students needed the help of friends and family to survive the internment, they depended upon each other to reveal it fifty years later in written form. Because the internment was a shared experience, the story of one student often related to that of another. As each student recalled a lost possession (Lesson 2), the stories accumulated into a catalogue of loss—a kitten, a puppy, a sword, a bicycle, a piano. In sharing these stories, each student was able to connect his or her narrative to a web of interconnected experiences. For the students, identification with one another's stories led to a heightened sense of individual and group empowerment.

III. Form, Point of View, and Theme

Each author's choice of form and point of view is governed, in part, by the nature of his or her memories. Some students were quite young at the time of the war and could not recall some of what had happened to them. "Create what you can't remember," I told the class. "Through other characters you can construct the past."

In "Owada's Market," Toru Saito steps back into 1942 through the fictional character of Mr. Owada, a Japantown grocer. Mr. Owada expresses the point of view of the many Issei who lost their businesses during the war.

Michi Tashiro's "Transformation of a Rice Sack" beautifully illustrates how some Issei replaced their lost possessions through the invention of new objects. Drawing upon the tradition of Japanese folklore, Michi brings us into the world of her mother—the character, Badger—who stitches a rice sack into an apron.

In her poem "The Rattlesnake and Scorpion," Ruth Y. Okimoto creates a dialogue between two animals who are confused by the construction of an internment camp in the place where they live. By inhabiting other voices, Ruth reinvents a historical moment. These characters allow us—the audience—to see how their habitat is taken over by manmade objects. This poem expresses the commotion Ruth felt during the incarceration, even if she cannot remember all of the details.

Over the course of our work, Michi found that the fairy tale was an appropriate medium for her to write her family history. In contrast, Toru and Ruth discovered that fictional characters were sometimes limiting. Like other class members who had experienced the internment as grade school children, or even as young adults, Toru and Ruth still held vivid memories, and they wanted to recapture them from their own points of view. For them, as with the majority of the class, autobiography was the primary *modus operandi*.

"This strategy is fine," I told the class. "Since you are writing family stories to be passed down, I respect that you want to stick to the facts. But sometimes the facts can get in the way and shut down your imagination. When forced to choose, you should always do what is best for your piece."

But this strategy also opened up other issues. For example, questions that arose during our discussions included: Is it acceptable to take creative license when writing about our experiences? What is "the truth" and what is our responsibility to it? Are their privacy issues when revealing the lives of others? Who is our audience?

Regardless of each student's position on such matters, the class agreed that a successful piece of writing was able to ground abstract themes such as separation and loss by carving concrete details into dramatic scenes. Yoshito Wayne Osaki builds narrative tension in "My Dog 'Teny'" when he recalls to us the day he and his family departed for camp and he was forced to leave his dog behind.

Another important decision each author had to make was where to position the narrator in relationship to other characters. Some stories use the first-person perspective to allow us to experience the narrator's compassion for others. Based on her observations as a child, Harumi Serata develops a catalogue of compelling characters, giving voice to the untold stories of certain detainees. In "Seatoru No Ojisan (Old Man From Seattle)," Harumi recalls how an internee in Minidoka waited day after day to be released back to his home, only to be sent to a mental hospital.

Much of the work locates us in a moment in the past and stays there. However, some pieces juxtapose different time frames. Florence Ohmura Dobashi's "Apple Butter" creates a dynamic relationship between past and present. Florence recalls how a specific food served at a social gathering triggers memories of camp, demonstrating how an unexpected circumstance can instantly conjure up camp life for any internee.

Like Florence, Kiku Hori Funabiki shows how her present day life is still informed by the internment in "Arthur." In speaking to a classroom full of inner-city children about the camps, Kiku illustrates how education can be a catalyst for social change.

By reading each author's section in *From Our Side of the Fence*, we are able to see how individual stories fit into a larger narrative arc. Characters recur. Plot lines overlap. We discern the changing relationship between each narrator and his or her family members over time.

Sato reminisces about the years before the war in "The Piano." When their mother dies, Sato and her sisters feel she is still close by because of the piano's presence. But when they are incarcerated, they must leave the piano behind. While they are able to remain emotionally close, Sato's family, like others, undergoes significant change. In "The Food" Sato does not sit with her brother or sisters in the detention center mess hall, and this new arrangement symbolizes to young Sato the breakdown of the family unit.

In certain passages, the first-person narrator grounds not only the particular details of a particular moment, but also relates the collective impact of a group experience. Florence Miho Nakamura recreates this type of moment in "Arrival in Tanforan" when she shows us how her family and others in her community were uprooted from their homes. In Fumi Manabe Hayashi's "Train Ride" she re-imagines, through the voice of a young child, the day she boarded the train for camp. Metaphorically, she gives us the frenzied inner monologue of any Japanese American child, her fears accumulating into a list of sad and desperate questions.

In Daisy Uyeda Satoda's "Segregation and the Loyalty Questionnaire," she shifts the narrative pronoun from "I" to "we" to demonstrate that, despite the divisive impact of the loyalty questions, her life and the lives of her peers merge into one. Although Daisy is referring to a specific place, time, and group of people, her story is a parable of all internees. It is a lament to and an accusation of America, the country that rounded up its own people, took them away from their homes, and penned them up.

IV. Revision

A major focus of the class was to develop the quality of each student's individual pieces and body of work. I wanted to help students to craft and polish their material, not temper their emotions or threaten the integrity of their voices. They needed to flourish on their own terms, not by any prescribed or unitary definition of what it meant to be a good writer. From my own experience as a writing student, I knew that an editor's or teacher's careless reading of one's work could be discouraging. While, on occasion, I was guilty of overediting, I kept an open channel of dialogue between the students and myself in order to avoid any possible misunderstandings.

Sometimes miscommunication arose from something as simple as penmanship. "I can't read your handwriting," a student might proclaim, pointing to a place that needed my translation. At other times communicating effectively was more complex. "What do you mean here?" a student might ask, waiting for me to clarify a point. If I had misunderstood something important in the student's piece, I would confirm that my comment was confusing or no longer useful. We would usually share a laugh over such exchanges, but serious learning took place too.

During the summer of 2000, I pored over the students' thick portfolios and selected their strongest work. While there was plenty of other powerful material I wanted to use, the process demanded trimming down.

As we dug into their pieces for the final time, the students displayed persistence. Their fierce drive to develop particular themes and subjects uncovered layer after layer of emotionally charged experience. In class and in our individual conferences, we detected problem areas and shared ideas about how to address them. We discussed how the ordering of narrative details affects a piece's dramatic movement; how syntax and grammar influence the flow and tone of a story; how diction can determine point of view. In the process of revision, students enhanced their writing with dialogue, concrete description, and personal details. Although the truth about internment was often painful, the students confronted it head on.

Now that *From Our Side of the Fence* is a finished product, my students and I would like it to provide an impetus for social change. We intend for this book to be a catalyst for other Japanese American communities to form their own writing groups. We also want it to reach those who are isolated, by geography or for any other reason, from other Japanese Americans. In following these lesson plans, any surviving internee can add to the stories collected in this book and the body of writing about the camps. Those once silent can now be heard.

— Brian Komei Dempster

Lesson 1 – Pearl Harbor

1) Where were you and what was your reaction when Pearl Harbor was bombed? How were you and your family affected? Did you get rid of symbols of your Japanese heritage? At school or elsewhere, how were you treated? Did you feel a need to show your "Americanness"?

Student Examples:
Florence Ohmura Dobashi, "After Pearl Harbor"
Sato Hashizume, "The Red, White, and Blue Badge"
Toru Saito, "Owada's Market" (an excerpt)
Daisy Uyeda Satoda, "Ganbare"

Recommended Reading:
Jeanne Wakatsuki Houston and James D. Houston, *Farewell to Manzanar*, Chapter 1: "What is Pearl Harbor?"
Charles Kikuchi, *The Kikuchi Diary*
Ellen Levine, *A Fence Away From Freedom*, Chapter 2: "Pearl Harbor"
Kazuo Miyamoto, *Hawaii: End of the Rainbow*, excerpt from *Only What We Could Carry* edited by Lawson Fusao Inada et al.
Monica Sone, *Nisei Daughter*, Chapter VIII: "Pearl Harbor Echoes in Seattle"
Yoshiko Uchida, *Desert Exile*, Chapter 3: "Pearl Harbor"
Yoshiko Uchida, *The Invisible Thread*, Chapter 12: "Becoming a 'Nonalien'"
Nellie Wong, "Can't Tell" from *The Open Boat* edited by Garrett Hongo

Lesson 2 – Lost Possessions

1) Make a list of possessions you and your family lost during the war. Try to concentrate upon those things which were the most intimate and meaningful to you—Was the piano you played sold? Did you lose your pet, your football, your favorite doll?

2) Choose an item from your list. What is the story behind this lost possession? How did you feel when you had to leave it behind? How and why did you miss it?

3) How did your relationship to this object change after the war? Does the loss of this object still affect you in the present?

Student Examples:
Sato Hashizume, "The Piano"
Fumi Manabe Hayashi, "Ashes"
Yoshito Wayne Osaki, "My Dog 'Teny'"

Recommended Reading:
Garrett Hongo, "Something Whispered in the *Shakuhachi*" from *Yellow Light*
Jeanne Wakatsuki Houston and James D. Houston, *Farewell to Manzanar*, Chapter 2: "Shikata Ga Nai"
Ellen Levine, *A Fence Away from Freedom*, Chapter 3: "On Orders from the President: Preparation for Evacuation"
Monica Sone, *Nisei Daughter*, Chapter VIII: "Pearl Harbor Echoes in Seattle"
Yoshiko Uchida, *Desert Exile*, Chapter 4: "Evacuation"

Film/Video:
John Esaki, *The Bracelet*
Emiko Omori, *The Departure*

Lesson 3 – Arrival

1) Do a freewrite upon the concept of arrival. What do you recall about the journey to the "assembly center" or "relocation center"? What images do you remember when you first arrived there? Take a step back into time. Enter into that moment again. What significant tastes, smells, and sounds did you encounter? Was there anything startling, compelling, surreal? What was your reaction? How did other family members react? Paint the picture as vividly as possible. Write whatever comes into your head. Don't edit your grammar and spelling.

Student Examples:
Sato Hashizume, "The Food" and "The Outhouse"
Fumi Manabe Hayashi, "Train Ride" and "Our Desert Home"
Florence Miho Nakamura, "The Living Room,"
    "Arrival in Tanforan," and "Barrack in Tanforan"
Toru Saito, "End of the Line"
Daisy Uyeda Satoda, "Tanforan Assembly Center"

Recommended Reading:
Jeanne Wakatsuki Houston and James D. Houston, *Farewell to Manzanar*, Chapter 2: "Shikata Ga Nai," Chapter 3: "A Different Kind of Sand," and Chapter 4: "A Common Master Plan"
Charles Kikuchi, *The Kikuchi Diary*
Ellen Levine, *A Fence Away from Freedom*, Chapter 4: "Life in the Camps"
Miné Okubo, *Citizen 13660*
Monica Sone, *Nisei Daughter*, Chapter IX: "Life in Camp Harmony"
Yoshiko Uchida, *Desert Exile*, Chapter 5: "Tanforan: A Horse Stall for Four" and Chapter 7: "Topaz: City of Dust"
Yoshiko Uchida, *The Invisible Thread*, Chapter 13: "Prisoner of My Country" and Chapter 15: "Topaz"
Mitsuye Yamada, *Camp Notes and Other Poems*

Film/Video:
Dianne Fukami and Donald Young, *Tanforan, Race Track to Assembly Center*
Robert Nakamura, *Something Strong Within*

Lesson 4 – Food

1) Describe your experience of the mess hall. Who did you eat with? How did your diet change? What were the most surprising and unusual foods you ate? Were any of these foods unpalatable? Are there any foods you were served in camp that you don't eat now?

Student Examples:
Florence Ohmura Dobashi, "Apple Butter"
Sato Hashizume, "The Food"
Michi Tashiro, "The Picnic"

Recommended Reading:
Sue Kunitomi Embrey et al., *Manzanar Martyr*
Catherine Embree Harris, *Dusty Exile*
Jeanne Wakatsuki Houston and James D. Houston, *Farewell to Manzanar*, Chapter 5: "Almost a Family"
Yoshiko Uchida, *Desert Exile*, Chapter 5: "Tanforan: A Horse Stall for Four" and Chapter 6: "Tanforan: City Behind Barbed Wire"

Lesson 5 – Interpreting Photographs

1) Describe a camp-related photograph or picture. What is happening? What are the concrete details you can use in order to paint the picture? Does the image trigger anything personal for you, any stories? Use the photograph as a springboard for your imagination.

Student Examples:
Kiku Hori Funabiki, "The Gap"
Fumi Manabe Hayashi, "Train Ride"
Ruth Y. Okimoto, "Magazine Pictures"
Michi Tashiro, "Transformation of a Rice Sack"

Recommended Reading:
Kimi Kodani Hill, *Topaz Moon*
James Masao Mitsui, "Destination: Tule Lake Relocation Center, May 20, 1942" and "Photograph of a Child, Japanese-American Evacuation, Bainbridge Island, Washington, March 30, 1942" from *The Open Boat*, edited by Garrett Hongo
Toyo Miyatake, *Toyo Miyatake*
Miné Okubo, *Citizen 13660*
Eiichi Edward Sakauye and Ernest Kazato, *A Reflection on the Heart Mountain Relocation Center*

Film/Video:
Steven Okazaki, *Days of Waiting*

Lesson 6 – Resourcefulness and Inventions

1) Did camp life force the adults to reinvent any lost possessions? Were you able to replace your favorite game or doll? Did you invent your own pretend world? Did you invent any games? How much did this invention compensate for your loss?

2) Did people make utilitarian household items (i.e., *geta*, clothing, furniture, etc.)? What materials did they use and where did they acquire them?

Student Examples:
Naoko Yoshimura Ito, "Letting Go" (quilt and caption)
Yoshito Wayne Osaki, "The Paper Christmas Tree"
Harumi Serata, "Fortune Telling"

Recommended Reading:
Ken Mochizuki, *Baseball Saved Us*
Yoshiko Uchida, *Desert Exile*, Chapter 5: "Tanforan: A Horse Stall for Four"

Lesson 7 – Arts and Crafts

1) What arts did internees create in camp? How did they express various forms such as *kabuki*, *ikebana*, and *bonsai*?

2) What crafts did internees create in camp? What types of decorations, accessories, jewelry, sculptures, etc., did internees make? What materials did they use and where did they find them?

Student Examples:
Harumi Serata, "Bitter Brush Story"
Michi Tashiro, "Transformation of a Rice Sack"

Recommended Reading:
Allen Hendershott Eaton, *Beauty Behind Barbed Wire*
Deborah Gesensway and Mindy Roseman, *Beyond Words*
Kimi Kodani Hill, *Topaz Moon*
Russell Leong and Karen Jacobson, eds., *The View from Within*
Toyo Miyatake, *Behind the Camera*
Miné Okubo, *Citizen 13660*

Film/Video:
Dianne Fukami, *Piecing Memories: Recollections of Internment*
Steven Okazaki, *Days of Waiting*

Lesson 8 – Holidays

1) How did you celebrate holidays and other special occasions in camp? What did you miss about the holidays back home? Did you invent any significant items you were unable to have in camp?

Student Examples:
Fumi Manabe Hayashi, "There's No Place Like Home"
Yoshito Wayne Osaki, "The Paper Christmas Tree"

Recommended Reading:
Chris Aihara and the Japanese American Cultural and Community Center, Los Angeles, *Nikkei Donburi*
Nancy Araki and Jane M. Horii, *Matsuri: Festival*
Yoshiko Uchida, *Desert Exile*, Chapter 8: "Topaz: Winter's Despair"
Yoshiko Uchida, *The Invisible Thread*, Chapter 18: "Concentration Camp Christmas"

Lesson 9 – Witness

Think about your position as a witness to any activity, character, or event which had a significant impact upon you. Choose from the following options:

1) Character

Write about any character whom you found compelling. Describe him or her in physical detail and your observations of them. What is his or her story? What effect did this person have upon you?

2) Privacy

Write about your living quarters. What did you hear through the walls? Were any activities or conversations revealed inadvertently? How did you overcome the lack of privacy?

3) Rumors

Write about any rumors or stories you overheard.

4) Parents

In camp, did any family member assume a different role? How did the relationship between family members change? What happened to the family structure?

Student Examples:
Florence Ohmura Dobashi, "The Blanket"
Sato Hashizume, "The Announcements"
Ruth Y. Okimoto, "The Rattlesnake and Scorpion"
Daisy Uyeda Satoda, "The Bath"
Harumi Serata, "Seatoru No Ojisan," "Obake Obasan," and "Rumors"

Recommended Reading:
Lawson Fusao Inada, *Legends From Camp*
Hiroshi Kashiwagi, "Laughter and False Teeth" from
    The Big Aiiieeeee! edited by Jeffery Paul Chan et al.
Janice Mirikitani, "Crazy Alice" from *Awake in the River*
Toshio Mori, "The Man with Bulging Pockets" from
    The Chauvinist and Other Stories
Hisaye Yamamoto, "The Legend of Miss Sasagawara" from
    Seventeen Syllables and Other Stories

Film/Video:
Veronica Ko, *Dear Miss Breed*
Emiko Omori, *The Departure*

Lesson 10 – The Loyalty Questionnaire

Internees who were seventeen years and older were forced to answer Questions 27 and 28 of the loyalty questionnaire.

Number 27: Are you willing to serve in the armed forces of the United States on combat duty, wherever ordered?

Number 28: Will you swear unqualified allegiance to the United States of America and faithfully defend the United States from any or all attack by foreign or domestic forces, and forswear any form of allegiance or obedience to the Japanese emperor, or any other foreign government, power or organization?

Answering "yes" or "no" to either question created irreversible consequences for all involved.

1) **For those of you who answered the loyalty questionnaire:**
   Freewrite upon your decision to answer "yes" or "no" to the questions. Did your family or friends play a significant role in your decision? What did you see as the positives and negatives of each choice? What were the consequences of your decision both during and after the war? Do you ever regret or second guess your decision? Why or why not?

2) **For those of you who did not answer the questionnaire:**
   Freewrite upon a family member or friend's decision to answer "yes" or "no." Did you witness any consequences of this choice? Did you notice division within and between families?

Student Examples:
Florence Ohmura Dobashi, "The Loyalty Questionnaire"
Yoshito Wayne Osaki, "The Loyalty Oath"
Daisy Uyeda Satoda, "Segregation and the Loyalty Questionnaire"

Recommended Reading:

Steven Chin, *When Justice Failed*

Jeanne Wakatsuki Houston and James D. Houston, *Farewell to Manzanar*, Chapter 11: "Yes Yes No No"

Hiroshi Kashiwagi, "The Betrayed" excerpt from *Only What We Could Carry* edited by Lawson Fusao Inada et al.

Ellen Levine, *A Fence Away from Freedom*, Chapter 8: "Resisters, No-Nos, and Renunciants"

David Mura, "The Blueness of the Day" from *The Colors of Desire*

John Okada, *No-No Boy*

Yoshiko Uchida, *Desert Exile*, Chapter 8: "Topaz: Winter's Despair"

Yoshiko Uchida, *The Invisible Thread*, Chapter 19: "Volunteers from behind Barbed Wire"

Michi Weglyn, *Years of Infamy*

Mitsuye Yamada, *Camp Notes and Other Poems*

Film/Video:

Frank Abe, *Conscience and the Constitution*

John DeGraaf, *A Personal Matter: Gordon Hirabayashi vs. the United States*

Loni Ding, *The Color of Honor*

Eric Paul Fournier, *Of Civil Wrongs and Rights: The Fred Korematsu Story*

Wendy Hanamura, *Honor Bound: A Personal Journey*

Steven Okazaki, *Unfinished Business*

Emiko Omori, *Rabbit in the Moon*

Scott Tsuchitani for the Tule Lake Pilgrimage Committee, *Meeting at Tule Lake*

Lesson 11 – Departure from Camp

1) Focus on your departure from camp. What were your anxieties about leaving old friends and family members?

2) What were your expectations of where you were going?

Student Examples:
Yoshito Wayne Osaki, "Leaving"

Recommended Reading:
Jeanne Wakatsuki Houston and James D. Houston, *Farewell to Manzanar*, Chapter 15: "Departures" and Chapter 17: "It's All Starting Over"
Toshio Mori, "The Travelers" from *The Chauvinist and Other Stories*
Yoshiko Uchida, *The Invisible Thread*, Chapter 20: "Back to the Real World"

Lesson 12 – Resettlement

1) Home

Focus on the resettlement period. Did you return to your former community or town? Did you have a home? Where did you stay? If you returned to your former home, how had it changed? Were objects missing? Were you faced with hostility? Was it difficult for you or your parents to find a job? What jobs did you or they have? How did you adjust to the various changes?

2) School

Describe your first day or week at school after leaving camp. What significant details and events do you remember? Did you have friends? Were you behind academically? Relate any incidents of racism.

Student Examples:

Kiku Hori Funabiki, "Return, But Not to My Backyard" (an excerpt)
Harumi Serata, "Ghost Story"

Recommended Reading:

Jeanne Wakatsuki Houston and James D. Houston, *Farewell to Manzanar*, Chapter 19: "Re-entry" and Chapter 20: "A Double Impulse"
Ellen Levine, *A Fence Away from Freedom*, Chapter 9: "Life Outside Camp"
Janice Mirikitani, "Tomatoes" from *Shedding Silence*
John Okada, *No-No Boy*
Monica Sone, *Nisei Daughter*, Chapter XI: "Eastward, Nisei" and Chapter XII: "Deeper into the Land"
Yoshiko Uchida, *The Invisible Thread*, Chapter 21: "From Mouse to Tiger" and Chapter 22: "Good Morning, Boys and Girls"
Mitsuye Yamada, "Cincinnati" from *Camp Notes and Other Poems*
Wakako Yamauchi, "The Sensei" and "Makapuu Bay" from *Songs My Mother Taught Me* edited by Garrett Hongo

Film/Video:

Dianne Fukami, *Starting Over: Japanese Americans After the War*

Lesson 13 – Silence

1) Did your parents ever discuss the camp experience with you? Did you ever speak to them about the camps? If you did have a conversation, relate this moment in the form of a vignette.

2) If you kept a diary in camp, what did it contain? If you ever discussed the camp experience with your children or others, describe this conversation in the form of a vignette.

3) Describe any incident that examines the relationship between racism and silence.

Student Examples:
Florence Ohmura Dobashi, "Racism and Silence"
Kiku Hori Funabiki, "Silence…No More"
Yoshito Wayne Osaki, "The Tackling Dummy"

Recommended Reading:
Joy Kogawa, *Obasan*
Janice Mirikitani, "Prisons of Silence" and "Breaking Silence" from
    Shedding Silence
John Tateishi, *And Justice for All*

Film/Video:
Stephen Holsapple and Satsuki Ina, *Children of the Camps*
Rea Tajiri, *History and Memory*

Lesson 14 – Redress

1) Participant

What was your role in the redress movement? What was your reaction to it? Did you testify? Why or why not? If so, describe the experience.

2) Observer

If you chose not to testify, did you still attend the redress hearings? Describe the atmosphere. What was your experience of listening to the testimonies? Did any particular story stand out for you? If so, write the story as you remember it and describe your emotional reaction.

Student Examples:

Kiku Hori Funabiki, "Silence…No More" and
    "Games 'Justice' Plays" (an excerpt)

Recommended Reading:

Ellen Levine, *A Fence Away from Freedom*, Chapter 10:
    "Setting Things to Rest"
Mitchell T. Maki et al., *Achieving the Impossible Dream*
John Tateishi, *And Justice for All*

Lesson 15 – Reunions and Visits to Camp Sites

1) Reunions
Have you attended a camp reunion? If so, why? What memories did it bring back? If you have not attended, what are the reasons?

2) Visits
Have you ever gone back to the camp site(s) where you were imprisoned? What recollections did it produce? What emotional impact did returning to the site have on you?

Student Examples:
Toru Saito, "Hidden Testimony"
Daisy Uyeda Satoda, "Topaz, 1993"

Recommended Reading:
Jeffery F. Burton et al., *Confinement and Ethnicity*
Frank Iritani and Joanne Iritani, *Ten Visits*
Tule Lake Committee and John R. and Reiko Ross, *Second Kinenhi*
Mitsuye Yamada, *Desert Run*

Film/Video:
Robert Nakamura, *Wataridori: Birds of Passage*
Scott Tsuchitani for the Tule Lake Pilgrimage Committee,
     Meeting at Tule Lake
Jesse Wine, *American Fish*

Lesson 16 – Legacies

1) Do you include your family at camp reunions and camp remembrances? Do you discuss with them the significance of those events?

2) How have you shared your internment story with those outside of your family, e.g. schools, organizations, media, etc.?

3) Describe any present-day experience that triggers a camp memory.

Student Examples:
Florence Ohmura Dobashi, "Apple Butter"
Kiku Hori Funabiki, "Arthur"
Florence Miho Nakamura, "Eucalyptus Trees"
Harumi Serata, "History II"

Recommended Reading:
Garrett Hongo, "Stepchild" from *Yellow Light*
Janice Mirikitani, "Generations of Women" from *Shedding Silence*
David Mura, "Gardens We Have Left" from *The Colors of Desire*
David Mura, "Prologue: Silences," "A Nisei Daughter," and
    "A Nisei Father" from *Where the Body Meets Memory*
Donna K. Nagata, *Legacy of Injustice*

Film/Video:
Justin Lin, *Interactions*
Corey Ohama, *Double Solitaire*
Rea Tajiri, *History and Memory*
Janice Tanaka, *Who's Going To Pay for these Donuts Anyway?*
Lisa Yasui and Ann Tegnell, *Family Gathering*

Annotated Bibliography

Recommended Reading for Lesson Plans

Aihara, Chris, and the Japanese American Cultural and Community Center, Los Angeles. *Nikkei Donburi: A Japanese American Cultural Survival Guide*. Chicago: Polychrome Publishing Corporation, 1999. A resource guide for the Japanese American family, which contains information about holidays, cultural traditions, foods, and crafts.

Araki, Nancy K., and Jane M. Horii. *Matsuri: Festival: Japanese American Celebrations and Activities*. South San Francisco: Heian International Publishing Co., 1978. This book describes various Japanese holidays: *Oshōgatsu* (New Year's); *Hinamatsuri* (Doll Festival/Girl's Day); *Tango No Sekku* (Boy's Day); *Tanabata* (Star Festival, 7th day of 7th month); *Bon Odori* (Bon dance).

Burton, Jeffery F., Mary M. Farrell, Florence B. Lord, and Richard W. Lord. *Confinement and Ethnicity: An Overview of World War II Japanese American Relocation Sites*. Tucson, Ariz.: Western Archaeological and Conservation Center, National Park Service, U.S. Department of the Interior, Publications in Anthropology 74, 1999. An overview of the remains of World War II Japanese American concentration and internment camp sites.

Chan, Jeffery Paul, Frank Chin, Lawson Inada, and Shawn Wong, eds. *The Big Aiiieeeee!: An Anthology of Chinese American and Japanese American Literature*. New York: Meridian, 1991. An anthology in which the editors have compiled selections of various Chinese and Japanese American writers.

Chin, Steven A. *When Justice Failed: The Fred Korematsu Story*. New York: Steck-Vaughn Company, 1993. This children's book dramatizes the struggles of Fred Korematsu, including his challenges to the government order of forced removal, his subsequent jailing and internment in Tanforan and Topaz, and decades later, his vindication in court.

Eaton, Allen Hendershott. *Beauty Behind Barbed Wire: The Arts of the Japanese in Our War Relocation Camps*. New York: Harper and Row, 1952. This book shows the ways in which internees turned to the creation of art during the years of their imprisonment.

Embrey, Sue Kunitomi, Arthur A. Hansen, and Betty Kulberg Mitson. *Manzanar Martyr: An Interview with Harry Y. Ueno*. Fullerton: California State University, Fullerton, Oral History Program, Japanese American Project, 1986. Transcripts of interviews with Harry Ueno, a mess hall cook in Manzanar concentration camp, who was sent to various jails and camps after he complained of a food shortage and other problems.

Gesensway, Deborah, and Mindy Roseman. *Beyond Words: Images from America's Concentration Camps*. Ithaca, N.Y.: Cornell University Press, 1987. A compilation of paintings, drawings, stories and commentaries from ex-internees that humanizes the incarceration experience.

Harris, Catherine Embree. *Dusty Exile: Looking Back at Japanese Relocation during World War II*. Honolulu: Mutual Publishing, 1999. The experiences and observations of a schoolteacher at the Poston War Relocation Center.

Hill, Kimi Kodani. *Topaz Moon: Chiura Obata's Art of the Internment*. Berkeley: Heyday Books, 2000. A book that presents the artwork of renowned painter Chiura Obata, researched and edited by his granddaughter, Kimi Kodani Hill.

Hongo, Garrett Kaoru. *Yellow Light.* Middletown, Conn.: Wesleyan University Press, 1982. Hongo's first volume of poems explores his family and cultural history, including the Japanese American internment, and pays homage to various landscapes.

Hongo, Garrett, ed. *The Open Boat: Poems From Asian America.* New York: Anchor Books, 1993. This anthology profiles the works of thirty-one emerging and established Asian American poets.

Houston, Jean Wakatsuki, and James D. Houston. *Farewell to Manzanar.* Boston: Houghton Mifflin Co., 1973. The memoir of a young woman's coming-of-age during the internment years.

Inada, Lawson Fusao. *Legends from Camp.* Minneapolis: Coffee House Press, 1993. A collection which contains poems about the internment and other significant historical events, as well as pieces inspired by jazz musicians and Asian American literary figures.

Inada, Lawson Fusao, Patricia Wakida, and William Hohri, eds. *Only What We Could Carry: The Japanese American Internment Experience.* Berkeley: Heyday Books, 2000. A collection of literature from the Japanese American internment experience, including poetry and fiction written and published in the camps, personal diaries and letters, memoirs of Japanese Peruvians, Hawaiians, and Italian Americans affected by the internment, as well as the recollections of African, Jewish, and other Asian American citizens who recall what was happening outside of the camps.

Iritani, Frank, and Joanne Iritani. *Ten Visits: Accounts of Visits to All the Japanese American Relocation Centers.* San Mateo, Calif.: Japanese American Curriculum Project, Inc., 1994. Using photographs, maps, and text, the authors document their visits to the sites of the ten Japanese American concentration camps.

Kashiwagi, Hiroshi. "Laughter and False Teeth." In *The Big Aiiieeeee!,* edited by Jeffery Paul Chan et al. New York: Meridan, 1991: 314-338. Set in an American concentration camp during World War II, and containing a cast of eccentric characters, this one-act play revolves around the theme of betrayal.

Kashiwagi, Hiroshi. "The Betrayed." In *Only What We Could Carry,* edited by Lawson Fusao Inada et al. Berkeley: Heyday Books, 2000: 270-278. In this excerpt from Kashiwagi's play, two characters, Grace and Tak, struggle with how to approach the issue of registration and the controversial loyalty questionnaire.

Kikuchi, Charles. *The Kikuchi Diary: Chronicle from an American Concentration Camp.* Edited by John Modell. Urbana: University of Illinois Press, 1973. Kikuchi's diary chronicles the period following the bombing of Pearl Harbor and his four-month stay at Tanforan Assembly Center.

Kogawa, Joy. *Obasan.* Boston: David R. Godine, 1982. A novel in which the main character, Naomi Nakane, examines the silence surrounding the Japanese Canadian internment experience, represented by the character of Obasan.

Leong, Russell, and Karen Jacobson, eds. *The View from Within: Japanese American Art from the Internment Camps, 1942-1945.* Los Angeles: Japanese American National Museum, UCLA Wight Art Gallery, and UCLA Asian American Studies Center, 1992. This exhibition catalogue profiles internee artists and supplements their artwork with essays, historical information, and vignettes.

Levine, Ellen. *A Fence Away From Freedom: Japanese Americans and World War II.* New York: G.P. Putnam's Sons, 1995. Levine's collected interviews of a group of Japanese Americans who reflect upon their lives before, during, and after the internment.

Maki, Mitchell T., Harry H.L. Kitano, and S. Megan Berthold. *Achieving the Impossible Dream: How Japanese Americans Obtained Redress*. Urbana and Chicago: University of Chicago Press, 1999. Using documents from archives, interviews, public statements, and various other research and writings, this book traces the evolution of the Japanese American redress movement.

Mirikitani, Janice. *Awake in the River*. San Francisco: Isthmus Press, 1978. Poetry and prose about the author's family history, their incarceration during World War II, and various contemporary issues.

Mirikitani, Janice. *Shedding Silence*. Berkeley: Celestial Arts, 1987. Containing poetry, prose, and a play, this book looks at cultural traditions, the intergenerational ties between women, and various historical atrocities, including the internment experience and the bombing of Hiroshima.

Mitsui, James Masao. "Destination: Tule Lake Relocation Center, May 20, 1942." In *The Open Boat: Poems From Asian America*, edited by Garrett Hongo. New York: Anchor Books, 1993: 198-199. This poem draws the vivid portrait of a woman being taken to a concentration camp.

Mitsui, James Masao. "Photograph of a Child, Japanese-American Evacuation, Bainbridge Island, Washington, March 30, 1942." In *The Open Boat: Poems From Asian America*, edited by Garrett Hongo. New York: Anchor Books, 1993: 200. In this poem, a child and his father are among a group of Japanese Americans who have been forced to leave their homes during World War II.

Miyamoto, Kazuo. "Hawaii: End of the Rainbow." In *Only What We Could Carry*, edited by Lawson Fusao Inada et al. Berkeley: Heyday Books, 2000: 180-190. This excerpt from Miyamoto's book looks at the impact of the bombing of Pearl Harbor on a Japanese American family in Hawaii.

Miyatake, Toyo. *Toyo Miyatake: Behind the Camera 1923-1979 (Miyatake Toyo No Shashin 1923-1979)*. Tokyo: Bungeishunju, 1984. A series of pictures Miyatake took with a box camera while he was incarcerated at Manzanar concentration camp, with accompanying text in Japanese.

Mochizuki, Ken. *Baseball Saved Us*. New York: Lee & Low Books Inc., 1993. This children's book chronicles a Japanese American boy's experience of playing baseball both inside and outside a concentration camp.

Mori, Toshio. *The Chauvinist and Other Stories*. University of California, Los Angeles: Asian American Studies Center, University of California, 1979. Short stories about the West Coast Japanese American community, set in the 1930s and 1940s.

Mura, David. *The Colors of Desire*. New York: Anchor Books, 1995. Mura's second volume of poetry looks at the internment and its legacies, as well as the relationship between issues of race, desire, and sexuality.

Mura, David. *Where the Body Meets Memory: An Odyssey of Race, Sexuality, and Identity*. New York: Anchor Books, 1996. In various sections of this book, Mura reflects upon the internment legacy passed down to him by his Nisei parents.

Nagata, Donna K. *Legacy of Injustice: Exploring the Cross-Generational Impact of the Japanese American Internment*. New York: Plenum Press, 1993. This study examines the impact of the internment upon Sansei whose Nisei parents were incarcerated.

Okada, John. *No-No Boy*. Seattle: University of Washington Press, 1979. A novel in which the main character, Ichiro, struggles with the consequences of having answered "no" to questions 27 and 28 of the loyalty questionnaire.

Okubo, Miné. *Citizen 13660*. Seattle: University of Washington Press, 1994. The author chronicles her life at Tanforan Assembly Center and Topaz War Relocation Center by pairing black and white drawings with vignettes.

Sakauye, Eiichi Edward, and Ernest Kazato. *A Reflection on the Heart Mountain Relocation Center: A Photo Essay*. San Mateo, Calif.: AACP, Inc., 2000. A journal of photographs and commentary on the Heart Mountain War Relocation Center.

Sone, Monica. *Nisei Daughter*. Boston: Little Brown and Co., 1953. The author contemplates what it means to be Japanese American before World War II, during her incarceration, and after her release from camp.

Tateishi, John, ed. *And Justice For All: An Oral History of the Japanese American Detention Camps*. New York: Random House, 1984. A collection of thirty oral histories that describe the incarceration.

Tule Lake Committee and John R. and Reiko Ross. *Second Kinenhi: Reflections on Tule Lake*. San Francisco: Tule Lake Committee and John R. and Reiko Ross, 1980 and 2000. This photo journal includes internee recollections of Tule Lake concentration camp and their accounts of return pilgrimages to camp sites.

Uchida, Yoshiko. *Desert Exile: The Uprooting of a Japanese-American Family*. Seattle: University of Washington Press, 1982. Drawing from real life experiences, Uchida describes her family's life before World War II as well as their uprooting and internment at Topaz.

Uchida, Yoshiko. *The Invisible Thread*. Englewood Cliffs, N.J.: Julian Messner, 1991. In Uchida's memoir she characterizes her family and school life in 1930s Berkeley, California, her internment at Topaz concentration camp, and her efforts to resettle into American society.

Weglyn, Michi. *Years of Infamy: The Untold Story of America's Concentration Camps*. New York: William Morrow & Co., 1976. A thoroughly researched and comprehensive account of the incarceration and the circumstances surrounding it.

Wong, Nellie. "Can't Tell." In *The Open Boat: Poems From Asian America*, edited by Garrett Hongo. New York: Anchor Books, 1993: 270. This poem offers a Chinese American perspective on the day Pearl Harbor was bombed.

Yamada, Mitsuye. *Camp Notes and Other Poems*. Latham, N.Y.: Kitchen Table: Women of Color Press, 1980. Poems about the internment and other subjects.

Yamada, Mitsuye. *Desert Run, Poems and Stories*. Latham, N.Y.: Kitchen Table: Women of Color Press, 1988. Poems and stories about landscapes, culture, identity, and history.

Yamamoto, Hisaye. *Seventeen Syllables and Other Stories*. Latham, N.Y.: Kitchen Table: Women of Color Press, 1988. Stories focusing on the lives of Japanese American women, both inside and outside the concentration camps.

Yamauchi, Wakako. *Songs My Mother Taught Me: Stories, Play, and Memoir*. Edited by Garrett Hongo. New York: The Feminist Press at the City University of New York, 1994. Yamauchi's collection tells the stories of Japanese American rural immigrants, tenant farmers, and factory workers before, during, and after the internment.

Recommended Film / Video for Lesson Plans

American Fish
Jesse Wine. 10 min./1995.
Based on the short story, "American Fish" by R.A. Sasaki, this unforgettable meeting between two women reveals their search to find a common past, which includes their concentration camp experience.
Distributor: NAATA, (415) 863-0814, www.naatanet.org/distrib

Beyond Barbed Wire
Terri DeBono and Steve Rosen. 57 min./1996. This film outlines the World War II battlefield accomplishments of the 100th Infantry Battalion/442 Regimental Combat Team by featuring stories recounted by Japanese Americans who fought in these segregated units to prove their loyalty to their country.
Distributor: NAATA, (415) 863-0814, www.naatanet.org/distrib

The Bracelet
John Esaki. 31 min./1990.
Intertwining historic footage and photographs with original illustrations, this video is based on Yoshiko Uchida's popular children's book about friends separated by war.
Distributor: Japanese American National Museum Media Arts Center, (800) 461-5266, www.janmmedia.org

Children of the Camps
Director: Stephen Holsapple, Producer: Satsuki Ina. 57 min./1999/ with study guide. This documentary captures the experience of six Japanese Americans who were confined as children in concentration camps and examines how this early trauma manifests itself in their adult lives.
Distributor: NAATA, (415) 863-0814, www.naatanet.org/distrib

The Color of Honor
Loni Ding. 90 min./1987.
Collective portrayal of Japanese Americans who wrestled with the contradiction of being incarcerated by their own government, yet being called to serve in its military in World War II.
Distributor: NAATA, (415) 863-0814, www.naatanet.org/distrib

Conscience and the Constitution
Frank Abe. 60 min./1999.
This film depicts a group of young Americans who were ready to fight for their country but resisted the draft, because the government refused to restore their rights as U.S. citizens and release their families from the concentration camps.
Distributor: Transit Media, (800) 343-5540, www.pbs.org/conscience

Days of Waiting
Steven Okazaki. 60 min./1988/with study guide. Academy-award winning documentary that depicts the story of artist Estelle Peck Ishigo, a Caucasian married to a Japanese American and incarcerated at Heart Mountain concentration camp, whose sketches and watercolors capture the struggle of internees to keep dignity and hope alive.
Distributor: NAATA, (415) 863-0814, www.naatanet.org/distrib

Dear Miss Breed
Veronica Ko. 15 min./1990.
The story of how a librarian became a hero to Japanese American youth in an American concentration camp.
Distributor: Japanese American National Museum Media Arts Center, (800) 461-5266, www.janmmedia.org

The Departure
Emiko Omori. 14 min./1983.
The film depicts the story of Haru, a young Japanese American girl growing up in California's Central Valley in the 1940s who, in dealing with the loss of her collection of Japanese dolls, comes to understand what it means to be Japanese American and an immigrant's daughter.
Distributor: NAATA, (415) 863-0814, www.naatanet.org/distrib

Double Solitaire
Corey Ohama. 20 min./1997.
This personal documentary uses the motif of games to look at how the internment affected the lives of two people, the filmmaker's father, Norm, and her uncle, Stan.
Distributor: NAATA, (415) 863-0814, www.naatanet.org/distrib

A Family Gathering
Lise Yasui and Ann Tegnell. 30 min./ 1988/with study guide. Beyond the inherited silence of her family's painful experience during World War II, Lise Yasui searches to understand her grandfather's past and its tie to her life.
Distributor: New Day Films, (212) 477-4604, www.newday.com

History and Memory
Rea Tajiri. 32 min./1991.
With scrolling texts, clips from Hollywood movies, historical objects, still photos and interviews with family members, this film shows Rea Tajiri's search to uncover her family's history and experiences in the Japanese American concentration camps.
Distributor: Video Databank (Chicago), (312) 899-5172, www.vdb.org

Honor Bound: A Personal Journey
Wendy Hanamura. 58 min./1995/ with study guide. The story of the 100th/442nd Regimental Combat Team as told from father, Howard Hanamura, to daughter, Wendy, fifty years later.
Distributor: National Japanese American Historical Society, (415) 921-5007, www.njahs.org

Interactions
Justin Lin. 26 min./1990.
This film chronicles four high school students as they are given four days to tackle one mission: to find out what life was like for teenagers in camp during World War II.
Distributor: Japanese American National Museum Media Arts Center, (800) 461-5266, www.janmmedia.org

Meeting at Tule Lake
Scott Tsuchitani for the Tule Lake Pilgrimage Committee. 33 min./1994. Created for the 1994 Tule Lake Pilgrimage, this video is the product of facilitated intergenerational discussion and "live" oral histories in which former internees share their experiences at the Tule Lake Segregation Center, a site for over 18,000 who were identified as "disloyals."
Distributor: NAATA, (415) 863-0814, www.naatanet.org/distrib

Of Civil Wrongs and Rights:
The Fred Korematsu Story
Eric Paul Fournier. 55 min./1999.
The film documents Fred Korematsu's quiet decision to resist the forced internment of Japanese Americans during World War II and his ultimate vindication thirty-nine years later.
Distributor: NAATA, (415) 863-0814, www.naatanet.org/distrib

A Personal Matter: Gordon Hirabayashi vs. The United States

John De Graaf. 30 min./1992/with study guide. This short film documents the experience of Gordon Hirabayashi, who refused to be interned on the grounds that Executive Order 9066 violated his Constitutional rights.
Distributor: NAATA, (415) 863-0814, www.naatanet.org/distrib

Piecing Memories: Recollections of Internment

Dianne Fukami. 17 min./2001. Using color, shape and imagery, the quilters at the Japanese American Services of the East Bay share their bittersweet memories of the internment through a quilt project entitled "Piecing Memories."
Distributor: Bridge Media, (510) 531-6906

Rabbit in the Moon

Emiko Omori. 87 min./1999. Uncovering a buried history of political tensions, social and generational divisions, and resistance and collaboration in the camps, director Emiko Omori shows her struggle against her own family's silence concerning the internment, in particular their amnesia about her mother, who died soon after her release from camp in Poston, Arizona.
Distributor: Transit Media, (800) 343-5540, www.newday.com/tmc/

Something Strong Within

Robert A. Nakamura. 40 min./1994. Featuring rare amateur film footage taken by internees, this film reflects the determination and strength of all Japanese Americans imprisoned in concentration camps during World War II.
Distributor: Japanese American National Museum Media Arts Center, (800) 461-5266, www.janmmedia.org

Starting Over: Japanese Americans After The War

Dianne Fukami for KCSM TV 60. 60 min./1996. This public television program documents the struggle of Japanese Americans as they resettled throughout the US after the war, fighting to overcome the stigma of being of Japanese ancestry and the prejudice they encountered as they tried to find housing and employment.
Distributor: NAATA, (415) 863-0814, www.naatanet.org/distrib

Tanforan, Race Track to Assembly Center

Dianne Fukami and Donald Young. 57 min./1995. Blending interviews, rare film footage, photographs and artwork, this film is the first in-depth study of an assembly center where thousands of Japanese Americans lived for as long as six months, while the more permanent World War II concentration camps were being built inland.
Distributor: NAATA, (415) 863-0814, www.naatanet.org/distrib

Unfinished Business

Steven Okazaki. 58 min./1986. This documentary tells the story of three Japanese Americans, Fred Korematsu, Gordon Hirabayashi, and Minoru Yasui, who were imprisoned for violating Executive Order 9066, fought their cases in court, and eventually overturned their original convictions.
Distributor: NAATA, (415) 863-0814, www.naatanet.org/distrib

Unforgettable Face

Nicole Newnham. 13 min./1993. In this documentary, George Oiye, one of the Japanese American soldiers who liberated prisoners from Dachau in 1945, and Yanina Cywinska, then a 16-year-old prisoner in the death camp, reunite almost fifty years after World War II.
Distributor: NAATA, (415) 863-0814, www.naatanet.org/distrib

Wataridori: Birds of Passage
Robert Nakamura, Visual
Communications. 37 min./1974.
The filmmaker paints the canvas of
four Issei who overcame hardship
and racism and, in one pilgrimage,
pay tribute to the memories of those
whose lives are forever imprinted
with the experiences at Manzanar.
Distributor: NAATA, (415) 863-0814,
www.naatanet.org/distrib

Who's Going To Pay for these
Donuts Anyway?
Janice Tanaka. 58 min./1992.
This video chronicles Tanaka's 50-year
personal search for her father, whom
she had not seen since age three and
whom she eventually finds in a halfway
house for the chronically mentally ill
in L.A.'s skid row.
Distributor: NAATA, (415) 863-0814,
www.naatanet.org/distrib

Websites

Bancroft Library of U.C. Berkeley
www.oac.cdlib.org/dynaweb/ead/calher/
jvac/
This archive houses many photographs
and documents relating to the internment
with an emphasis on Bay Area Japanese
American experiences.

DENSHŌ
Japanese American Legacy Project
www.densho.org
This site offers background information
about the Denshō Archive, which
includes live action interviews with
transcripts, as well as articles and
photographs about the Japanese
American experience.

Exploring the
Japanese American Internment
www.jainternment.org
Through a rich body of film and audio
clips, photos, poetry, stories and
interactive activities, this site allows
viewers to meet the survivors of the
internment "face to face."

NAATA Distribution
www.naatanet.org/distrib
This catalogue of nearly 200 video
and film titles on the Asian American
experience offers on-line rental or
purchase for institutional use; and
selected titles for individual home
purchase by phone or email.
Tel: (415) 552-9550,
Email:distribution@naatanet.org

National Archives
www.nara.gov/nara/searchnail.html
A collection of documents, immigration
files, and photo archives from the War
Relocation Authority records relating to
the Japanese American internment.

National Japanese American
Historical Society
www.njahs.org
Dedicated to the collection, preservation,
authentic interpretation, and sharing of
historical information about the Japanese
American experience, NJAHS has
developed this website to inform the
diverse national community about its
events, publications, and exhibitions, and
to serve as a resource for those interested
in Japanese American history.

Concentration Camps, Assembly Centers & Isolation Centers[2]

Detention Centers (small type) were hurriedly constructed while the ten more permanent concentration camps (bold face) were being built. Internees spent approximately six months at these temporary holding facilities. The ten larger camps were all located inland from the coast.

WASHINGTON

Puyallup Fairgrounds

Portland Exposition Hall

MONTANA

Missoula Isolation Center

OREGON   IDAHO

HEART MOUNTAIN

MINIDOKA

WYOMING

TULE LAKE

NEVADA   UTAH

Marysville
Sacramento
Tanforan
Stockton
Turlock
Merced   Pinedale
Salinas
Fresno
Tulare   **MANZANAR**

CALIFORNIA

Santa Anita
Pomona

TOPAZ

COLORADO

Moab
Isolation Center

AMACHE •

ARIZONA

Leupp
Isolation Center

Mayer

POSTON

GILA RIVER

ARKANSAS

ROHWER •

JEROME •

Shaded area:
Internment zone

America's Concentration Camps for Japanese Americans during World War II[1]

(Listed in order of their establishment)

Center Name/Location	Opening Date	Closing Date	Peak Resident Population
Manazar Manzanar, Inyo Cty, Ca.	Mar. 21, 1942	Nov. 21, 1945	10,046
Colorado River Poston, Yuma Cty, Az.	May 8, 1942	Nov. 28, 1945	17,814
Tule Lake Newell, Modoc Cty, Ca.	May 27, 1942	Mar. 20, 1946	18,789
Gila River Rivers, Pinal Cty, Az.	July 20, 1942	Nov. 10, 1945	13,348
Minidoka Hunt, Jerome Cty, Id.	Aug. 10, 1942	Oct. 28, 1945	9,397
Heart Mountain Heart Mountain, Park Cty, Wy.	Aug. 12, 1942	Nov. 10, 1945	10,767
Granada Amache, Prowers Cty, Co.	Aug. 27, 1942	Oct. 15, 1945	7,318
Central Utah Topaz, Millard Cty, Ut.	Sept. 11, 1942	Oct. 31, 1945	8,130
Rohwer McGehee, Desha Cty, Ark.	Sept. 18, 1942	Nov. 30, 1945	8,475
Jerome Denson, Drew/Chicot Cties, Ark.	Oct. 6, 1942	June 30, 1944	8,497

[1] Table source: United States Department of Interior, *WRA: A story of human conservation*, Washington, D.C., 1946: 197, *et passim*. Originally titled: "War Relocation Centers for Japanese Americans during World War II."

[2] Map Source: *The Price of Prejudice* by Leonard Arrington, 1997: 17. Originally titled: "Federal Internment Camps, Assembly Centers & Isolation Centers." Used with permission by Ted Nagata. U.S. Department of Justice Camps not included.

Note: The War Relocation Authority also maintained, during the first four months of 1943, a temporary isolation center near Moab, Utah, and between April and October, 1943, the Leupp Isolation Center, Winslow, Arizona. From March 1944 to 1946, it also operated the emergency shelter for 1,000 European war refugees at Fort Ontario, Oswego, New York.

OPPOSITE TOP: April 29, 1942. Panorama of Salinas detention center. Internees were held first in detention centers before being assigned to concentration camps further inland. Clem Albers, WRA phtograph, National Archives at College Park.

Glossary of Terms

Japanese words and phrases

bonsai – the Japanese art of dwarfing trees; a dwarfed tree
enryo – deference, constraint, reserve
gaman – endurance
giri – obligation
ikebana – Japanese flower arrangement
kabuki – Japanese classical theatrical drama
oyatsu – snacks
shoganai – colloquialism for *shikata ga nai*, it cannot be helped

Japanese American generational distinctions

Issei – first-generation Japanese immigrants
Nisei – second-generation Japanese American
Sansei – third-generation Japanese American
Yonsei – fourth-generation Japanese American
Kibei – born in America and educated in Japan
Nikkei – person of Japanese ancestry

Historical references

assembly centers – Temporary detention centers that housed Japanese Americans who had been forcibly removed from the West Coast in the early months of World War II. These "assembly centers" were hastily erected quarters located throughout California and the West at fairgrounds, racetracks, and other similar facilities.

Civil Liberties Act of 1988 – enacted on August 10, 1988, to redress the wrongs committed by the United States government toward Japanese Americans during World War II. The Civil Liberties Act of 1988 called for a formal apology written by the president and $20,000 in compensation for each survivor of America's concentration camps.

concentration camps – Euphemistically called "relocation centers" by the War Relocation Authority (WRA), the concentration camps were hastily constructed facilities for housing Japanese Americans forcibly removed from their homes and businesses on the West Coast during World War II. Located in isolated areas of the U.S. on either desert or swampland, the camps were usually surrounded by barbed wire and guarded by armed sentries. Most inmates were transferred to their camp by train from an "assembly center" between April and September 1942. In all, over 120,000 Japanese Americans served time in these camps. Tule Lake concentration camp in California was the last of the camps to be closed in March 1946.

Day of Remembrance – The Day of Remembrance is an annual ceremony held on or around February 19 in most major cities with significant Japanese American populations to commemorate the signing of Executive Order 9066. The first Day of Remembrance was held in 1978 in Seattle, Washington.

evacuation – refers to moving people in order to rescue and protect them from danger. Flood, hurricane, and earthquake victims are evacuated and relocated. The government used "evacuation" as a euphemism to refer to the forced removal of the Japanese Americans during World War II.

Executive Order 9066 – signed by President Franklin D. Roosevelt on February 19, 1942, authorized the War Department to "prescribe military areas . . . from which any or all persons may be excluded." This order, which on the surface made no reference to Japanese American or native-born Japanese, served as the basis for the future curfew and "exclusion orders" issued by Lt. General John L. DeWitt and the mass incarceration of all West Coast Japanese Americans in concentration camps.

internment camps – were administered by the Justice Department for the detention of enemy aliens deemed dangerous during World War II. While the majority of the approximately 120,000 Japanese Americans who were incarcerated during World War II were in one of the ten concentration camps administered by the War Relocation Authority (WRA), several thousand others came under the jurisdiction of the Justice Department in a separate and parallel internment. Reflecting the usage of terms in most recent historical literature, the WRA camps are referred to as "concentration camps" while the Justice Department camps are called "internment camps."

Redress Movement – Movement organized by the Japanese American community in the 1970s and '80s to obtain an apology and compensation from the United States government for its wrongful actions towards them during World War II. This movement resulted in the Civil Liberties Act of 1988.

relocation centers – Euphemism used by the government for the ten permanent WRA camps.

War Relocation Authority (WRA) – Governmental agency charged with administering America's concentration camps. The WRA was a civilian agency created by Executive Order 9012 on March 18, 1942, to oversee the detention of Japanese Americans during World War II.

All historical references are taken, with permission from the Japanese American National Museum, from Japanese American History: An A-to-Z Reference from 1868 to the Present, *Brian Niiya Editor. Japanese American National Museum, 1993.*

Credits

Production Team
Editor: Brian Komei Dempster
Production Manager: Jill Mari Shiraki
Designer: Zand Gee
Outreach Coordinator: Kimberly Ina
Events Coordinator: Ken Maeshiro
Photo Archivist: Sevenju Pepper
KSW Staff: Nancy Hom and Claire Light

Special Acknowledgments:
Patricia Wakida, Heyday Books
Cameron Trowbridge, Japanese
    American National Museum
Charlie Hinton, Inkworks Press
Julie Hatta, National Asian American
    Telecommunications Association
John Tateishi, National Japanese
    American Citizens League
Rosalyn Tonai, National Japanese American
Historical Society
Zand Gee, photographer
Sevenju Pepper, photographer
Richard Wada, photographer

Project Support

Vida Benavidas	Alina Hua
Brenda Cárdenas	Roy Kamada
Tina Chang	Manami Kano
Sabina Chen	David Kim
Edmond Chow	Sue Kwock Kim
Grace Sin-Yee Chow	Riyad Koya
Jason Chu	Daniela Kuper
Jay Ruben Dayrit	Cynthia Madansky
Loren Kiyoshi	Dard Neuman
Dempster	Patrick Phillips
Renko Dempster	Anastasia Royal
Stuart Dempster	Steven Salchak
Merrill Feitell	Nancy Satoda
Estévan Rael Y	David Shih
Gálvez	Audrey Shoji
Jennifer Grotz	Grace Talusan
Kristin Henderson	James Tjoa
Michael Honch	Marc Wallis
Lillian Howan	

Credits/Permissions
*Growing Up Nisei: Images of Japanese American
Culture, 1920s to 1950s, Japanese American
National Museum 1997 Calendar.* May:
"Dances," Gift of Asami and Eiji Fukumoto
(94.196); Yumi Hara (96.97.1); Harry, Shigeru
and Shozo Iba (89.55); Dr. and Mrs. Masy
Masuoka (92.109); Mei Nakano (98.174.3);
the Takeuchi Family (94.292); and Yoshiko

(Hosoi) Sakurai Collection (94.183), Japanese
American National Museum. Photography by
Norman H. Sugimoto. June: "Magazines,"
Gift of Mr. John S. Nitta, Japanese American
National Museum (95.145). Photography by
Norman H. Sugimoto.

Map illustration: "Federal Internment Camps,
Assembly Centers & Isolation Centers" from
The Price of Prejudice by Leonard J. Arrington,
Delta, Utah: The Topaz Museum, 1997, p. 17.
Courtesy of Ted Nagata.

**California Civil Liberties Public Education
Program (CCLPEP)** was created through
legislation known as the California Civil
Liberties Public Education Act, or AB1915
(Chapter 570 Statutes of 1998), which was
introduced by Assemblymember Mike Honda
of San Jose. The purpose of the CCLPEP
is to provide competitive grants for the
development and implementation of public
educational activities and materials in order
to ensure that the events surrounding the
exclusion, forced removal, and incarceration
of U.S. citizens and permanent resident aliens
of Japanese ancestry will be remembered.
The intent is also to illuminate and
understand the causes and circumstances of
this and similar events. For more information
about the CCLPEP, contact the
California State Library at (916) 653-9404
or www.library.ca.gov/cclpep

**Japanese Cultural & Community Center
of Northern California (JCCCNC)** is a nonprofit organization that was envisioned by the
community to promote and preserve its
Japanese American ancestry, cultural heritage,
histories, and traditions. JCCCNC strives to
meet the diverse multi-ethnic and generational needs of the community by offering
affordable services, usage of its facility, and
programs in culture, the arts, and education.
For information, contact: www.jcccnc.org

Kearny Street Workshop (KSW) is a
multi-disciplinary Asian Pacific American arts
organization that serves the Asian Pacific
American community by presenting programs
that address its concerns, encouraging artistic
expressions, and honoring its historical and
cultural heritage. For information, contact:
www.kearnystreet.org